Bold Prayers

How to Pray with Confidence and Expectation

By
Clarence E. Stowers, Jr.

Copyright 2024 Clarence E. Stowers, Jr. All rights reserved.

ISBN- 979-8-88940-547-4 (Cloth)
ISBN- 979-8-88940-542-9 (ePub)

Printed in USA by Staten House Italics in Scripture quotations are the author's emphasis.

Unless otherwise indicated, Scripture quotations are from: Holy Bible: New Living Translation. Wheaton, IL: Tyndale House Publishers, 2004. Used by permission.

This book may not be reproduced in any form or by any means, including electronic and mechanical storage systems, without the author's written consent, except for brief excerpts quoted by reviewers.

Although the author and publisher have made every effort to ensure that the information in this book was correct at press time, the author and publisher do not assume and hereby disclaim any liability to any party for any loss, damage, or disruption caused by errors or omissions, whether such errors or omissions result from negligence, accident, or any other cause.

This publication is designed to provide accurate and authoritative information with regard to the subject matter covered. It is sold with the understanding that the publisher is not engaged in rendering professional services. If legal advice or other expert assistance is required, the services of a competent professional should be sought.

The fact that an organization or website is referred to in this work as a citation and/or a potential source of further information does not mean that the author or the publisher endorses the information the organization or website may provide or recommendations it may make. Please remember that Internet websites listed in this work may have changed or disappeared between when this work was written and when it is read.

Bold Prayers

How to Pray with Confidence and Expectation

Table of Contents

Preface 1
   Transformative Power of Prayer 1
   Cultivating Confidence asnd Expectancy 1
   Inclusive Approach 2
   Your Invitation to Inspiration 2

What makes this book different than other books on prayer? 3
   Focus on Confidence and Expectancy 3
   Personal Insights and Experiences 3
   Practical Tips and Guidance 4
   Broad Range of Topics 4
   Emphasis on the Transformative Power of Prayer 4

The Purpose of Discussion Questions 6
   Personal reflection 6
   Group discussion 6
   Writing prompts 6

Introduction 8

Chapter 1: Discover the Power of Bold Prayer 12
   Abraham Prayed Boldly 15
   Denzel Washington Prayed Boldly 18
   Infusing Prayer with Faith 22
   Expanding Your Prayer Focus 22
   Persevering Through Silence 22
   Digging into the Word 23
   Cultivating Gratitude 23
   Praying in Jesus' Name 23
   Seeking the Spirit's Guidance 23

    Embracing Surrender 23
    Joining in Community Prayer 24
    Anticipating Answers 24
    Chapter One Discussion Questions 24
    Take Action 26

Chapter 2: Overcome Your Fear of Asking for Big Things 28
    Hannah's Prayer 31
    Rosa Parks' Prayer 34
    Chapter Two Discussion Questions 38
    Take Action 40

Chapter 3: How To Pray With Confidence and Expectation 43
    Elijah Prayed With Confidence and Expectation 46
    Martin Luther King Prayed With Confidence And Expectation 49
    Chapter Three Discussion Questions 53
    Take Action 55

Chapter 4: Pray For Bold Breakthroughs In Your Finances 57
    Job's Breakthrough Prayer 61
    Fredrick Douglass's Breakthrough Prayer 64
    Chapter Four Discussion Questions 68
    Take Action 69

Chapter 5: Praying Boldly for Your Marriage and Family 72
    Priscilla and Aquila Prays Boldly 75
    Jimmy and Rosalynn Carter Prays Boldly 78
    Chapter 5 Discussion Questions 82
    Take Action 83

Chapter 6: Praying Bold for Strong Leadership, Wisdom, and Commitment to Prayer 86

    Daniel Prays Boldly for Strong Leadership,
Wisdom, and Commitment to Prayer 89
    Dr. Benjamin Mays for Strong Leadership, Wisdom,
and Commitment to Prayer 93
    Chapter Six Discussions 96
    Take Action 98

Chapter 7: Adapting to New Challenges 100

Chapter 8: Being Open to Change and Growth 104

Chapter 9: Building on Ancient Wisdom for
Modern Day Success 108

Appendix A: Resources for Further Study 112
    Books 112
    Online Courses and Workshops**Error! Bookmark not defined.**
    Podcasts 113
    Communities 115

Appendix B: Reflection Questions for Personal
or Group Study 116
    Individual Reflection 116
    Group Study Discussion 117

Appendix C: Templates for Personal Prayer 119
    Template 1: Prayer for Personal Growth 119
    Template 2: Prayer for Overcoming Challenges 120
    Template 3: Prayer for Wisdom and Guidance 120
    Template 4: Prayer for Family and Loved Ones 120
    Template 5: Prayer for Leadership and Influence 121

Preface

In this journey, I am eager to share not just knowledge but experiences—those profoundly personal moments when prayer touched the core of my soul and re-shaped my understanding of faith and connection with God. Prayer is a profound dialogue, an intimate exchange with the Divine. It's where we bare our souls, express our deepest yearnings, and await God's boundless grace. In these pages, I will dive deep into this sacred communication, inviting you to explore its full potential alongside me.

Transformative Power of Prayer

Each chapter within this book will shine a light on a different facet of prayer's transformative potential. From healing to manifesting breakthroughs, you will see how prayer can shift your life. Imagine a prayer that changed the course of my life, providing clarity amidst chaos and peace within turmoil. I want to share these experiences with you. I'm going to show you not just how to pray, but why.

Cultivating Confidence and Expectancy

To pray with confidence and expectancy is to believe in the promise of divine response. I'm going to show you how to do that.

Inclusive Approach

These pages are crafted for you, whether you are a seasoned believer or newly curious about the power of prayer. I am committed to inclusivity, ensuring that each insight and instruction resonates, offering a welcoming hand into the world of faithful dialogue with God.

Your Invitation to Inspiration

Let this Preface be more than an introduction; let it be an invitation—a call to explore the vast expanse of prayerful communication. I am here to inspire, guide, and share in the remarkable journey that prayer unveils.

As we turn these pages together, I expect you to open your heart, engage with the narratives and practices within, and embark on a transformative path of prayer that seeks and expects divine encounter and intervention.

With warm regards and prayerful anticipation,

Clarence E. Stowers Jr.

What Makes This Book Different Than Other Books on Prayer?

BOLD PRAYERS: How to Pray with Confidence and Expectation is the must-have resource for anyone seeking to deepen their faith and relationship with God through prayer. While there are many books available on the subject of worship, BOLD PRAYERS stands out in several key ways:

Focus on Confidence and Expectancy

One key thing that sets BOLD PRAYERS apart is its focus on confidence and expectancy in prayer. Many books on prayer address the matter of faith, but I examine the specific topic of praying with confidence and expectancy. I explore the biblical foundations of confidence and expectancy in prayer and offer practical tips and guidance for cultivating these attitudes.

Personal Insights and Experiences

Another critical aspect of BOLD PRAYERS is the personal nature of the content. I share my insights and experiences with prayer and use these to illustrate essential points and encourage readers in their journey. Readers can truly grasp the essence of a book's authenticity and teaching style when they feel a personal connection to it.

Practical Tips and Guidance

BOLD PRAYERS provides biblical foundations and personal insights, and it also offers practical tips and guidance for praying with confidence and expectancy. These tips range from studying the Word of God and seeking advice from a pastor or counselor to practicing gratitude and seeking prayer partners. Readers can apply the book's concepts to their lives in a tangible way by following these practical steps.

Broad Range of Topics

BOLD PRAYERS covers a wide range of topics related to prayer. It addresses the most important aspects of prayer, including praying for healing and deliverance, praying for bold financial breakthroughs, praying for marriages and families, and experiencing the miraculous through worship. This book is useful for many readers and appeals to people from various walks of life because it emphasizes the transformative power of prayer.

Emphasis on the Transformative Power of Prayer

Prayer is not just a way to communicate with God; it is also a way to experience His love and presence personally and intimately. This emphasis on the transformative power of prayer helps readers see the value of prayer beyond just asking for things or seeking guidance.

BOLD PRAYERS: How to Pray with Confidence and Expectation is a unique and valuable resource for anyone seeking to deepen their faith and relationship with God through prayer.[1] This book is different. It focuses on confidence and expectancy, personal insights and experiences, practical tips and guidance, a broad range of topics, and the transformative power of prayer.

---

[1] Look What God Is Doing - Dick Eastman.
https://dickeastman.com/books/look-what-god-is-doing/

The Purpose of Discussion Questions

Discussion questions at the end of each chapter prompt readers to engage with the material, reflect on the chapter's teachings, and apply them to their own experiences. There are a few different ways to use discussion questions::

Personal reflection

One way to use discussion questions is to reflect on them individually and consider how the chapter's teachings apply to your life. These questions can help you think more deeply about the material and identify areas where you might need to grow or change.

Group discussion

Another effective way to leverage discussion questions is through group discussions. Whether it's a book club, church group, or your friends and family, engaging in these conversations will lead to fresh insights and a broader understanding of the chapter's teachings.

Writing prompts

Use discussion questions as writing prompts. This method is a powerful tool for processing the material and reflecting on your thoughts and feelings. Writing about your responses will help you gain clarity and a deeper understanding of how the chapter's teachings apply to your life.

It doesn't matter how you use the discussion questions. The goal is to engage with the material and consider how it applies to your life. By reflecting on the questions and discussing them with others, you will better understand the chapter's teachings and how they can help you grow in your faith and relationship with God.

Introduction

Do you ever feel like your prayers bounce off the ceiling and never reach God? Do you struggle with uncertainty or fear when praying for big things? If so, you are not alone. Many believers need more confidence and expectation in their prayer lives.

In the heartwarming introduction to "Bold Prayers," we are immediately welcomed into a communal space of shared experiences and vulnerabilities. Here, the struggles of prayer life are not only acknowledged but deeply understood and addressed. This book is a beacon of hope, offering insights and a journey toward transforming our communication with the divine.

Imagine an intimate conversation about prayer that does not shy away from the doubts, fears, and feelings of unworthiness that so many of us grapple with. The introduction sets the stage for this dialogue, reaching out with empathy and compassion, inviting us into a shared exploration of what it means to pray boldly and expectantly.

To further enrich this encounter, we propose weaving in compelling, real-life testimonies from diverse individuals. These stories will illustrate the concept of bold prayer and demonstrate that this approach to prayer is timeless, acutely relevant, and accessible to all. Each narrative should highlight a unique challenge or doubt, followed by the transformative experience of embracing bold prayer.

Readers will gain connection and inspiration from these stories.

To demystify the concept of "bold prayers," we must provide a clear, accessible definition early in the text. This definition should be illuminated by a poignant example or a brief yet vivid narrative that brings this idea to life. This definition will act as a guiding light, helping readers navigate the book's content with a clear understanding of its foundational message.

Furthermore, a preview of the practical strategies and tools that the book offers would significantly enhance reader engagement and anticipation. Outlining these resources not only sets expectations but also builds excitement for the actionable guidance to come. This sneak peek could introduce a framework or methodology that will be explored in subsequent chapters, encouraging readers to actively engage with the material and apply it to their own prayer lives.

By interweaving these elements into the introduction, we transform it from a mere opening section into a profound invitation. This invitation is not just to read but to participate in a transformative process, to join a community of believers who are journeying together toward more meaningful, empowered prayer practices.

As we dig into the book, readers will find each chapter building upon the last, creating a comprehensive guide to cultivating a bold prayer life. The book is designed to be both progressive and inclusive, addressing readers at various stages of their spiritual journey. The book makes a clear and compelling case for the power of prayer to effect change—not just internally but in our external circumstances as well. It draws on a wealth of testimonies and scriptural references to demonstrate how prayer can overcome obstacles, achieve breakthroughs, and experience divine intervention.

Another crucial theme is the idea of partnership with God through prayer. This partnership is characterized by trust, dialogue, and co-creation. It invites readers to view prayer not as a one-sided request but as a collaborative process with the divine. The book offers insights into developing this partnership, fostering a deeper connection with God, and aligning our prayers with divine will.

The concept of transformation through prayer is also a significant focus. Readers are encouraged to view prayer as a dynamic, transformative practice that can reshape their perceptions, intentions, and actions. The book provides clear guidance on embracing prayer as a catalyst for personal growth and spiritual evolution. It highlights the transformative potential of praying with intention, focus, and openness to change.

In addition to these thematic elements, the book is imbued with practical advice, exercises, and reflections designed to deepen the reader's understanding and practice of bold prayer. These resources are intended to be actionable and impactful, enabling readers to integrate the principles of bold prayer into their daily lives.

Throughout the journey, the book emphasizes the importance of community, sharing, and mutual support in the practice of prayer. Readers are encouraged to connect with others, share their experiences, and build a supportive network that enriches their prayer life.

In closing, the introduction to "Bold Prayers" serves as a heartfelt call to embark on a journey of discovery and transformation. It invites readers to explore the depths of their prayer life, embrace the power of bold, expectant prayer, and experience the profound impact it can have on their relationship with God and their overall well-being.

As you, the reader, turn these pages and engage with the insights and practices shared, we are certain that you will find not only knowledge and guidance but also inspiration, connection, and a renewed sense of purpose in your prayer life. Embrace the adventure of bold prayer and step into a future filled with faith, empowerment, and divine connection.

Chapter 1:
Discover the Power of Bold Prayer

So, you want to pray boldly?

In this chapter we will explore the concept of bold prayer and how it can transform our lives. We will look at biblical examples of bold prayer and its power to bring about miraculous change. We will also consider the role of faith and expectation in bold prayer and how these attitudes can help us to pray confidently and trust in God's goodness and plans. So let's dive in and discover the power of intercessory prayer together! In "Chapter 1: Discovering the Power of Courageous Prayer," we will explore what it means to pray courageously and how it can transform our lives.

First, let's define courageous prayer. Bold prayer is simply a prayer that is full of faith, confidence, and expectation. It is a prayer that is not afraid to ask God to do great things, knowing that He is able to do immeasurably more than we can ever ask or imagine (Ephesians 3:20). Bold prayer is not about being presumptuous or demanding, but rather about trusting in the goodness and power of God and His ability to work in our lives.

Praying boldly isn't about being presumptuous. It's not about manipulating God. Instead, it is about aligning ourselves with His plans and purposes. Praying boldly means following His lead and being obedient to His will.

It takes faith to pray boldly. It takes faith and trust in God to fulfill what He has promised. It also requires confidence in ourselves and our ability to pray together. Praying boldly means stepping out in faith and joining God in His work, rather than just asking for something.

Expectation is necessary for bold prayer. We must believe that God will answer our prayers. Although we won't always get what we ask for, we can trust God to work out His purposes. We can be confident that God will hear us and answer for us when we pray boldly.[2]

One of the great examples of bold prayer in the Bible is Abraham. Abraham is known as the "Father of Faith" because of his willingness to trust God and follow Him wherever He led. This is seen most clearly in his prayer for the people of Sodom and Gomorrah. When God told Abraham that He would destroy the wicked cities, Abraham interceded on their behalf, asking God to spare them if only a few righteous people lived there (Genesis 18:23-33). This was a bold prayer because Abraham was asking God to change His mind about His plans for the cities.

Genesis 18:23-33 records Abraham's bold prayer for the people of Sodom and Gomorrah. In this passage, God tells Abraham to destroy Sodom and Gomorrah because of their sin and corruption. Abraham asks God to spare the cities if only a few righteous people live there in response to this news.

---

[2] Blog Archives - Messiah Missionary Baptist Church.
https://www.messiahmbcpon.com/from-the-pastors-desk/archives/12-2021

In this prayer, Abraham asked God to change His mind about the cities. Abraham believed that God is just and righteous, and that there must be some righteous people in Sodom and Gomorrah who deserve to be spared. He prayed boldly, trusting that God would hear him and respond as he saw fit.

While God didn't spare the cities in the end, Abraham's bold prayer shows us the power of intercession. The story also emphasizes the importance of trusting God and his goodness, even when his plans seem unclear.

But Abraham's boldness in prayer didn't end there. In Genesis 15, God made a covenant with Abraham, promising to give him and his descendants the land of Canaan. However, Abraham and his wife Sarah were childless at the time, and fulfilling God's promise seemed impossible.

But Abraham believed God's promise and prayed for a son, even though it seemed humanly impossible (Gen 15:2-6). Through Abraham's faith and bold prayer, Isaac was born, fulfilling God's promise and becoming the ancestor of countless believers. Therefore, let's pray boldly, trusting in God's goodness and interceding for others. We should have faith and expect God to hear and respond to our prayers.

Abraham Prayed Boldly

Abraham stands as a monumental figure in the tapestry of faith, demonstrating the power of bold prayer. His dialogue with God over the fate of Sodom demonstrates not only his boldness, but also his intimacy with the Almighty. This section explores Abraham's boldness in prayer and offers insights into how we can apply such boldness to our modern spiritual lives.

As described in Genesis, Abraham's encounter with God wasn't a monologue but a lively conversation. He didn't passively accept God's plans. Instead, he engaged, questioned, and negotiated. Imagine the scene: Abraham, standing before the Creator of all, daring to ask, "Will you really sweep away the righteous with the wicked?" His boldness in questioning God's justice is both shocking and illuminating.

This story is instructive. Abraham's boldness didn't come from disrespect, but from deep faith and understanding of God's character. He knew that God was just, compassionate, and willing to engage with his creation. This should encourage us to approach God with our comprehensive questions and bold requests rooted in an understanding of His nature.

What's more, Abraham's prayer was not self-centered. His boldness was on behalf of others, pleading for the lives of the righteous in Sodom. This aspect of his prayer challenges us to expand our prayer lives beyond our own needs and to intercede fervently for others. It's a call to shift our focus outward, to intercede for justice and mercy.

But how do we bring such boldness to our prayers today? The first step is to cultivate a relationship with God in which such dialogue is possible. Abraham's boldness came from his close walk with God, a relationship built over years of trust and obedience. It's a reminder that bold prayer comes from deep spiritual connections.

In addition, understanding God's character and promises is critical. His knowledge of God's righteousness informed Abraham's boldness. We, too, must immerse ourselves in Scripture, learning who God is and what He desires for us and the world. Such understanding empowers our prayer by aligning our requests with His will.

Authentic faith, characterized by bold prayer, is not silent. It speaks, acts, and engages with the divine. Abraham's story calls us to a dynamic and conversational faith. It's a call to shed timid prayers and adopt a posture of confidence before God, knowing that He welcomes our boldness.

But bold prayer also requires humility. Abraham approached God acknowledging that he was "but dust and ashes. This balance of boldness and humility is crucial. It acknowledges God's sovereignty while exercising our privilege to speak openly with Him. Such humility doesn't weaken our prayer; it strengthens it, making it a true act of faith.

Emulating Abraham's boldness means stepping out in faith even when the outcome is uncertain. It's about big, bold prayers, trusting not in our power but in God's ability to do immeasurably more than we can ask or imagine. It's about not limiting God with our fears or insecurities, but allowing Him to work miracles.

Interestingly, Abraham's prayer also teaches us about acceptance. Despite his bold intercession, the fate of Sodom was not ultimately changed. This outcome illustrates that bold prayer is not about changing God's will to fit ours, but about aligning our hearts with His, even when His answers differ from our desires. It's about trust, surrender, and faith in His perfect plan.

Applying Abraham's boldness in our prayers means regularly stepping into areas of discomfort where our faith is stretched. It may mean praying for something that seems impossible, standing in the gap for others, or simply being honest with God about our doubts and fears.

Abraham's example inspires us to pray boldly for transformation, justice and mercy in our communities. We are called not to be passive believers, but active intercessors who boldly bring the needs of our world before God, trusting in His power to bring about change.

The legacy of Abraham's bold prayer extends far beyond his time. It sets a precedent for us, encouraging us to break out of the confines of timid prayer. His story guides us toward a prayer life of courage, zeal, and deep commitment to God.

As we reflect on Abraham's boldness, let's be inspired to cultivate such boldness in our prayers. His example encourages us to approach God with confidence, to bring our bold requests before Him, and to intercede passionately for others. In doing so, we deepen our relationship with God and become instruments of His will on earth.

In conclusion, Abraham's bold prayer is a call to action for us. It's an invitation to enter into a deeper, more honest dialogue with God in which our prayers reflect our needs and the desires of His heart for humanity. By praying

---

[3] "How Prayer—and His Mother—Kept Denzel Washington Humble | the Oprah Winfrey Show | OWN." *Www.youtube.com*, youtu.be/lR8R2KDi2g4?si=CfGFoL7kf50z_jgv. Accessed 3 May 2024.

boldly, we align ourselves with God's transformative power and become catalysts for his love and justice.

Denzel Washington Prayed Boldly

Denzel Washington is known for his powerful performances in films like Training Day and Fences. He is also known for his deep faith and commitment to prayer. In interviews, Washington has spoken about the importance of prayer and how it has helped him get through difficult times and make important decisions.[3]

In a world hungry for real stories of faith and courage, Denzel Washington's story stands out. It's a testament to the power of bold and unwavering prayer. An acclaimed actor and deep believer, Washington's journey underscores a deeply personal relationship with faith, where prayer is not just a ritual, but a vibrant, living dialogue with the Divine.

Washington once told an interviewer that he prays for wisdom, especially before embarking on a new project or making important life decisions. This practice of boldly asking for guidance mirrors the biblical Solomon and underscores the timeless relevance of seeking divine wisdom. Washington's prayers aren't quiet whispers, but fervent, passionate pleas made with the expectation that they will elicit a holy response.

His boldness in prayer extends beyond personal gain. Known for his generosity, Washington roots his acts of kindness in a life of prayer. He believes in the transformative power of prayer not only to change individual lives, but also to impact communities and the world at large. This reflects the concept that bold prayer leads to bold action, a recurring theme that resonates deeply with believers and seekers alike.

Among his many testimonies, Washington recounts a moment when prayer changed the trajectory of his career, leading him to roles with deeper meaning. This reflection points to an essential aspect of bold prayer: aligning one's life with divine purpose. By praying boldly, Washington opens himself to divine orchestration, willing to be led to places he hadn't imagined.

Another fascinating facet of Washington's prayer life is his belief in the power of intercession. He often mentions praying for himself and others, understanding the collective strength found in praying for one another. This act underscores an important principle of courageous prayer: it's as much about others as it is about ourselves. Intercessory prayer expands our focus from our needs to the needs of others, creating a ripple effect of faith and hope.[4]

Washington's story is also a poignant reminder that courageous prayer requires faith in adversity. He recounts times of uncertainty and challenge, moments when the outcome seemed bleak. Yet it was in these valleys that his prayer life deepened, proving that courageous prayer thrives not only in moments of victory, but also in times of trial.

Washington also emphasizes the importance of gratitude in prayer. He often began and ended his day with thanksgiving, a practice that rooted his life in an attitude of humility and appreciation. Gratitude, he demonstrates, is a powerful component of courageous prayer because it

---

[4] *Understanding the True Purpose of Giving: The Joy in Generosity*. 21 July 2023, houseoftheharvest.org/giving/purpose-of-giving/.

acknowledges the many ways God moves in our lives, often in the most unexpected ways.

The sincerity of Washington's prayer life challenges the modern skeptic. In a world often cynical about the power of faith, his testimony shines as a beacon of hope, affirming that prayer is not an outdated practice but a vital, life-giving force.

For those seeking to deepen their prayer life, Washington's example serves as a practical guide. He encourages believers to approach God with honesty, fervor, and expectation. Whether seeking guidance, interceding for others, or expressing gratitude, his life illustrates that prayer, when offered boldly, can indeed move mountains.

This chapter explores Denzel Washington's story and extracts practical lessons that readers can apply to their own lives. It challenges readers to elevate prayer from a mundane routine to a dynamic conversation with God, understanding that each prayer whispered in faith reflects a heartbeat aligned with the divine.

As we dig deeper into bold prayer, let us be inspired by Washington's journey. His story is not just about the accomplishments and accolades, but about a man who dared to pray boldly, to trust completely, and to live a life rooted in unwavering faith. It's about the transformative power of prayer that, much like the story of Nehemiah, can usher in a renewal from rubble to revival.

In conclusion, Denzel Washington's prayer life embodies the essence of boldness: asking with conviction, walking by faith, and embracing the fullness of God's plan with open arms. By following his example, we, too, can discover the profound impact of bold prayer on our spiritual journey. It's a journey marked by divine guidance, deepened faith, and an unwavering commitment to seeing God's hand in every aspect of our lives. So let us pray boldly, with hearts ready to receive and hands ready to do the work that prayer calls us to do.

As we move into the next chapter, we carry with us the inspiration and lessons of Washington's life. It's a foundation upon which we can build our understanding of prayer, not as a last resort or a wish list, but as a deep dialogue with the Creator who invites us to ask, seek, and knock with boldness and faith. Let us move forward with the courage to respond to this call, transforming our prayer life and, as a result, our lives.

As we embark on a journey of bold prayer, we are inspired by the steadfast faith of Abraham and the contemporary example of Denzel Washington. Their examples illuminate a path where faith is active, dialogical, and deeply rooted in trust and relationship with God.

Infusing Prayer with Faith

Think of your prayers as seeds planted in fertile soil, nourished by your faith in God's goodness and power. Imagine what it means to believe that God can do "immeasurably more" (Ephesians 3:20). It's about letting that truth settle deep in your heart and transform the way you approach God with your requests and dreams.

Expanding Your Prayer Focus

While personal petitions are essential, let's take a broader perspective and pray earnestly for others. Consider the transformative impact your intercession could have on the lives around you, reflecting a heart that reflects God's compassion and concern for all of His creation.

Persevering Through Silence

When heaven seems silent, remember the enduring faith of Abraham, who trusted God's timing and purpose. Embrace patience as a companion to faith, knowing that together they weave a stronger fabric of spiritual resilience.

Dive into the Word

Let Scripture be your daily bread, nourishing your soul and strengthening your faith. As you immerse yourself in God's promises and character, your prayers will naturally grow in confidence and alignment with His will.

Cultivate Gratitude

Approach God with a thankful heart, acknowledging the blessings and lessons interwoven throughout your life. This attitude of gratitude uplifts your spirit and positions you to receive more of God's goodness.

Pray in Jesus' Name

Remember the profound privilege of approaching God through Christ. Praying in Jesus' name is a powerful affirmation of your identity and authority as a believer, increasing your confidence in prayer.

Seek the Spirit's Guidance

Accept the Holy Spirit as your prayer partner, guiding you to pray in harmony with God's heart and purposes. His gentle nudging can transform your prayer life from routine to revelatory.

Embrace Surrender

Boldness in prayer involves the humility to submit to God's better plan. It's about holding our desires loosely, willing to exchange them for His perfect will, and saying with a trusting heart, "Thy will be done."

Joining in Community Prayer

Collective prayer is a unique power where faith comes together and is strengthened. Whether in a church, a small group, or a prayer trio, find your spiritual tribe and journey together in bold prayer.

Anticipating Answers

When you embrace these practices, you're not just reciting words into the void; you're entering into a dynamic relationship with the Creator, one that invites you to speak, listen, and act with courage and conviction. As we absorb these lessons and integrate them into our daily lives, our prayer becomes a vibrant, life-changing dialogue marked by earnest expectation and heartfelt devotion.

So let's approach God's throne with the boldness exemplified by Abraham and Denzel, carrying our prayers with faith, enthusiasm, and the full assurance that we are heard and loved. In doing so, we not only draw closer to God's heart, but also step into our role as co-creators of a reality infused with His grace and truth.

Chapter One Discussion Questions

After immersing yourself in the compelling stories of Abraham and Denzel Washington, each of which illustrates the profound impact of bold prayer, it's time to reflect on how their stories resonate with your own spiritual journey.

The purpose of these questions isn't just to ponder theoretical possibilities, but to catalyze a transformation in your prayer life. Engaging with these questions can act as a bridge, connecting the inspiration of these stories to your journey toward spiritual empowerment.

1. **Reflect on your current prayer habits.** Consider the boldness of your prayers in light of Abraham's and Denzel Washington's stories. Have you held back in your requests to God, perhaps out of fear or unworthiness? Compare your current approach to prayer with the boldness shown in these stories. What practical steps can you take to begin praying more boldly and expectantly?

2. **Identify the barriers.** What personal barriers or beliefs have kept you from praying boldly? These could range from a lack of faith to a fear of disappointment or even misconceptions about what is "appropriate" to ask of God. Consider how these barriers have shaped your prayer life and brainstorm strategies for overcoming them. How can you dismantle these barriers to open up a more dynamic, trusting relationship with the divine?

3. **Envision the impact of bold prayer in your life.** Imagine the changes that could occur in your life if you began to pray with the boldness of Abraham and Denzel Washington. How might your circumstances, relationships, or personal growth be changed? Visualize the potential results and use this as motivation to increase your prayer practice. What specific area of your life most needs the intervention of bold prayer right now?

Engaging deeply with these questions opens the door to a revitalized prayer life where bold requests are met with divine responses in ways you may never have anticipated. Remember, the journey to deeper, more effective prayer is a process. It builds on each act of faith, no matter how small. Let the stories of Abraham and Denzel Washington serve as a beacon to guide you to the untapped potential in your prayers. Your courage to ask boldly could be the catalyst for miraculous change, setting the stage for a story of renewal that mirrors Nehemiah's ancient yet timeless story of faith.

Take Action

In discovering the power of bold prayer, it is critical to move from insight to action. Understanding the stories of Abraham and Denzel Washington demonstrate the profound impact of stepping out in faith with boldness in prayer. These stories are not just tales of the past, but invitations to engage in a transformative practice in our lives. To truly embrace the lessons of bold prayer, we must go beyond the pages of this book and integrate these principles into our daily routines.

First and foremost, identify an area in your life that needs a bold prayer. It could be a personal challenge, a dream you've been holding back from pursuing, or an impossible situation. Allow yourself to be vulnerable and admit where you most need divine intervention. This honesty is the first step to bold prayer; it is the foundation for miracles to unfold.

Next, commit to praying daily for that concern, but with a twist. Approach your prayer with the same boldness that Abraham and Denzel Washington demonstrated. This means praying with expectation, not hesitation. It's about believing in the possibility of the unlikely, with faith that your prayers will be heard and answered, though perhaps not in the way you expect. Remember, bold prayer is not about demanding, but about humbly yet confidently presenting your desires to the Divine.

In addition, keep a journal of your bold prayer journey. Record your thoughts, feelings, and any changes in your situation. This will serve as a tangible reminder of your commitment and help you see the ways, large and small, that your prayers are impacting your life. Reflecting on these entries over time can strengthen your faith and encourage you to continue to pray boldly.

Finally, share your experiences with others. Praying boldly is not only a personal endeavor, but also a communal one. By sharing your journey, you inspire others to embark on their own adventures in faith. Whether in a small group, with a friend, or in a larger community setting, sharing your experience can magnify the power of bold prayer, creating ripples of faith and transformation far beyond what you can imagine.

Chapter 2:
Overcome Your Fear of Asking for Big Things

Embarking on a journey to deepen one's prayer life begins with understanding the true nature of prayer. It's not just a list of wishes whispered into the void or a ritual recitation, but a bold, raw, and intimate dialogue with the divine. In this sacred discourse lies the power to transform - spiritually and in our daily, tangible reality. Yet many tremble at the thought of asking for much, held back by fear and a sense of unworthiness.

Why are we afraid to ask for more? The answer, complex in its simplicity, revolves around our inherent vulnerability. To ask boldly is to expose our deepest desires and fears, to stand naked with our needs, hoping not to face rejection or indifference. But our hesitation reflects our limited understanding of the nature of the divine, not the divine itself.

Consider Hannah's fervent prayer for a child - a story explored further in this chapter. Her story testifies to the power of persistence and is a beacon of hope for those who feel their prayers are too bold. Her journey from despair to fulfillment reminds us that it is not the magnitude of our requests that intimidates the Divine. Instead, it's in the audacity of our prayers that our faith is tested and strengthened.

Rosa Parks' prayer for courage and justice in a time of rampant inequality didn't whisper into the void; it roared, igniting a movement that changed the course of history. Their story underscores that courageous prayers, not just personal petitions, can catalyze societal transformation.

Overcoming this fear begins with unwavering faith- faith that empowers us to knock on heaven's gates with our prayers, confident that we'll be heard. It's about understanding that our worthiness is not a currency we earn to connect with the divine.

Embrace vulnerability as strength. When you allow your authentic self to stand before the Divine and ask for your true desires, you transcend the barriers of fear and step into infinite possibilities where your requests are felt, not just heard.

Visualization increases faith and prepares your mind to receive. Imagine the fulfillment of your prayers in vivid detail. Feel the emotions and immerse yourself in the joy of receiving. Surrounding yourself with answered prayer stories and biblical or personal testimonies acts as a pillar of hope, reminding you of the power of bold prayer.

Prayer is partnership. Asking for big things doesn't mean dictating terms, but entering into a co-creative process where your actions are aligned with the requests. This partnership is built on trust-trust that even if the answer is "no" or "wait," it's woven into a larger tapestry of goodness.

Commit to gratitude. It shifts your focus from scarcity to abundance, making receiving big things more accessible to believe.[5] Gratitude cultivates an open, receptive heart.

Debunk the myth that asking for great things signifies greed or selfishness. When aligned with purpose and the greater good, your prayers carry a resonance that transcends self-interest and acknowledges the boundless generosity of the Divine.

Let go of unworthiness. Remember that the Divine's generosity isn't rationed according to merit, but reflects unconditional love and grace. You're invited to approach the Divine not as a beggar, but as a beloved child.

Finally, take action. Faith without works is stagnant. Show commitment by taking steps toward your request, no matter how small. This demonstrates faith and prepares you to receive.

As we set out together, let's throw off the shackles of fear and embrace the liberation of bold prayer. Let's dare to ask for desires that ignite our souls, knowing that we are heard, loved, and capable of receiving far beyond our imagination. Here's to asking big, to renewal through prayer, and to the unfolding stories of transformation.

Hannah's Prayer

Embarking on a journey to deepen one's prayer life begins with understanding its essence - a bold, raw, and intimate dialogue with the divine that holds transformative power. Yet many are paralyzed by fear when it comes to asking for monumental things, shackled by doubt and a

---

[5] Manifestating What You Want. C – Michele Blood – Enlightenment. https://micheleblood.com/manifestatingwhatyouwantc/

sense of unworthiness. The biblical figure of Hannah confronted this fear head-on.

Hannah's plight was a deep, soul-deep longing to be a mother. Year after year, she faced not only barrenness but also societal scorn as her unfulfilled desire clashed with cultural expectations of progeny. She was asking for nothing less than a life-changing miracle-the kind that often paralyzes us because the greater the request, the more insurmountable the obstacles seem.

But Hannah's approach teaches humility and perseverance. Her prayer was not a demand, but a surrender, a vulnerable pouring out of her soul before the Lord. She boldly admitted her inability to change her circumstances, trusting instead in her ability and God's ability. This attitude challenges the notion that surrender is defeat; instead, it acknowledges that some victories require divine intervention.

Notice the specificity of Hannah's plea for a son-a clarity that reflects her unwavering belief that God cares about the details of life. Her vow to dedicate this child to the Lord's service underscores her understanding that answered prayers have a purpose beyond personal joy. Though Eli the priest initially mistook her for a drunk, his eventual blessing reassured Hannah, just as spiritual authorities can uplift in the midst of doubt.

Hannah's face changed before her prayer was manifested, illustrating how the sincere presentation of requests to God changes our perspective and instills peace regardless of the immediate outcome. When Samuel was born, it taught patience and trust in divine timing-our requests may not manifest immediately, but they are in alignment with a better plan.

Hannah then fulfilled her vow, underscoring that bold prayers carry commitments beyond our desires. Her story illustrates that such boldness comes from faith, humility, and patience-asking with conviction, surrendering fully, waiting eagerly, and responding faithfully.

As we reflect on Hannah's example, we are invited to examine our approach. Do we hold back bold requests out of fear of disappointment or disbelief in the possibility? Her story encourages us to overcome trepidation and approach God with humble boldness rooted in unwavering trust.

But Hannah is not the only example of bold prayer in the midst of adversity. Rosa Parks' journey underscores how petitions rooted in faith can catalyze social change. As we weave their stories together, we find a tapestry of personal triumph and spiritual determination that sparks far-reaching change. Their paths converge on this truth: courageous prayers have the power to alter individual trajectories and reshape collective realities.

Through their stories, we learn that bold petitions spring from unwavering faith, humble surrender, and the understanding that some victories require divine partnership. Yet their boldness came not from arrogance, but from clarity of purpose and conviction of God's sovereignty.

Just as Hannah dared to ask for something profoundly life-changing after years of barrenness, Rosa Parks' prayer for courage in the midst of injustice ignited a movement that changed the course of history. In both, we see the paradoxical strength of vulnerability-of acknowledging limitations while holding on to the promise of divine capacity.

Their stories remind us that courageous prayer involves a request and a commitment to align our actions with the fulfillment of that request. Just as Hannah vowed to dedicate Samuel, Rosa's life became a living testament as she consistently chose the courageous path in the face of ridicule.

In addition, these stories illustrate the perseverance required when bold requests seem unanswered. Hannah yearned for years, and the road to justice for Rosa and her contemporaries was arduous. Yet their perseverance flowed from a deep inner peace-a change of countenance that comes not after the desired outcome, but in the very act of surrender.

Courageous prayer thus reveals itself as a transaction and a transformative process. Asking reshapes us, waiting refines faith, and receiving opens new vistas of purpose and service. Whether personal or societal, monumental prayers ripple far beyond the initial request.

So as we strive to breathe new depth into our prayer lives, may we find inspiration in the courage of Hannah and Rosa Parks. May their examples encourage us to abandon self-imposed limitations and approach the throne of grace with bared hearts and emboldened spirits, for it is in the boldness of our petitions that we honor the boundless divine grace and potential.

The path before us beckons an attitude of humility and an unshakeable conviction that our prayers shape unseen realities. May we ask boldly, wait patiently, and receive graciously, allowing each prayer to touch our character and the tapestry of human events?

Rosa Parks' Prayer

In Chapter 2: Overcoming Your Fear of Asking for Big Things, we explore the transformative nature of prayer, vividly illustrated through the life of Rosa Parks, a linchpin of the civil rights movement. Her pivotal act of defiance on a Montgomery bus was not an impulsive outburst, but a manifestation of deep, prayerful conviction. Known as the "Mother of the Freedom Movement," Rosa Parks' prayer life exemplifies how bold appeals to the divine can catalyze personal and societal transformation.[6]

Rosa Parks' journey underscores that prayer is more than a private monologue; it is an intimate communion with the divine, capable of influencing the granular realities of our daily lives and the broader tapestry of society. Her unwavering reliance on prayer for courage and guidance embodies the conviction that bold petitions to God can produce monumental results. In the midst of adversity and societal upheaval, her unwavering faith, strengthened by prayer, exemplifies the power of turning to God in personal turmoil and seeking justice and equity for all.

Her story teaches that prayer should not be limited to individual desires, but should be expanded to include larger visions for justice, equality, and community well-being. The boundless scope of prayer that Rosa Parks embraced encourages us to expand our petitions beyond our immediate concerns to advocate for transformative change in our communities and beyond.

---

[6] The Parks - Germantown Inn.
https://germantowninn.com/suites/the-parks/

In emulating such profound faith, we learn that approaching God with significant requests is not about assuming guaranteed outcomes, but cultivating trust in His ultimate wisdom and timing. Rosa Parks exemplifies that while immediate answers may elude us, each prayer sows a seed that is destined to flourish in its appointed time under divine providence.

In addition, her story underscores the importance of community support in one's prayer journey. Rosa Parks was not an isolated supplicant; her prayers were interwoven with a broader faith community, reflecting a collective resonance of spiritual strength and mutual uplift. This communal aspect of prayer illustrates that while our petitions are personal, their ripple effects can inspire, energize, and mobilize collective efforts for justice and peace.

Consider the following ways to cultivate a prayer life that reflects the boldness of Rosa Parks and other champions of faith:

1. **Engage in Faith-Filled Prayer:** Anchor your petitions in an unwavering belief in God's omnipotence, trusting that He can orchestrate outcomes beyond our wildest dreams.

2. **Cultivate Vulnerability with God:** Approach God genuinely, sharing your innermost fears, desires, and uncertainties. In this way, vulnerability can be transformed into a bridge to deeper spiritual intimacy.

3. **Exhibit Perseverance:** Persevere in prayer efforts even when divine silence seems pervasive. Embrace patience, recognizing it as a testament to your faith and a pathway to spiritual maturity.

4. **Root Your Prayers in Gratitude:** Cultivate a heart of gratitude, acknowledging the blessings you have received and shifting your perspective from scarcity to abundance.
5. **Pray in Community:** Participate in collective prayer initiatives, drawing on shared beliefs and aspirations to strengthen your faith journey and contribute to community uplift.

As we reflect on the profound legacy of Rosa Parks, we are challenged to expand our prayer horizons and dare to make significant, transformative requests, not just for personal gain, but for the greater good. Inspired by their unwavering commitment to justice, made possible through prayer, we too are invited to harness the power of prayer to champion causes greater than ourselves.

Engaging in such bold prayer aligns us with a venerable tradition of faith warriors like Rosa Parks, whose stories inspire and challenge us to imagine a more expansive, impactful prayer life. This narrative urges us to step forward in faith, to present our bold petitions and earnest expectations, and to be ready to witness the divine orchestrate profound transformations in our lives and society.

When we boldly present our visions and desires to God, we trust and surrender to an ancient covenant. This faith acknowledges our dependence on a power far greater than our own and invites divine intervention in impossible matters.

By adopting a bold and courageous approach to prayer, we can become more than mere petitioners. We become active participants in a divine dialogue, working alongside the Almighty to create a reality filled with justice, mercy, and grace. Our prayers then become powerful instruments of change that resonate through time and space, shaping our destiny and the legacy we leave for generations to come.

Therefore, let us embrace this sacred calling with humility and boldness, recognizing that our deepest longings, when placed before the Divine, are powerful catalysts for change. Drawing inspiration from the courage and conviction of figures like Rosa Parks, let us walk our path in prayer, marked by enthusiasm, resilience, and an unwavering belief in the miraculous.

In this journey of prayerful boldness, we are not alone. We stand shoulder to shoulder with a great cloud of witnesses, past and present, who have dared to dream, to ask, and to believe in the face of adversity.[7] As we venture forward, let us carry their legacy forward, encouraged by the knowledge that our prayers, no matter how great, resonate with a divine ear attuned to our most resounding cries and aspirations.

So as we chart our course through this chapter and beyond, let's throw off the shackles of fear and embrace the liberating power of bold prayer. Let's dare to articulate what we believe is attainable and what ignites our passion, knowing that in the sacred act of asking, we align ourselves with a divine agenda that far exceeds our imagination. Here's to a life of prayer that dares to ask, believes in

---

[7] They Didn't Want You to Know This: The Armor of God Explained Like Never Before! - Victorious in Prayer.
https://victoriousinprayer.com/they-didnt-want-you-to-know-this-the-armor-of-god-explained-like-never-before/

receiving, and rejoices in the transformative journey of faith.

Chapter Two Discussion Questions

Beginning the journey of asking for big things, especially in prayer, can often feel daunting. It's not just about making requests; it's an intricate dance of faith, courage, and surrender. As we explore this transformative process, let's pause and reflect. Here are some thought-provoking questions to deepen your understanding and guide your practice:

1. **How does the fear of asking for big things in prayer reflect broader fears in your life?**

    Have you noticed similarities between your reluctance to pray and other instances of holding back? Do you think your reluctance stems from a fear of being disappointed, feeling unworthy, or perhaps not believing that change is possible? Spend some time thinking about this, as it may reveal certain beliefs that are hindering your prayer life and personal growth.

2. **Recall a time when you witnessed a bold prayer being answered.**

    Sometimes seeing is believing. Think of a time, either in your own life or in the life of someone close to you, when a bold prayer was answered in a remarkable way. How did this experience affect your faith and prayer practice? Was there a shift in your perspective of what's possible through worship?

3. **What "big thing" do you hold back from asking for in your prayers, and why?**

Identify something significant that you've been reluctant to bring before God in prayer. Explore the reasons for your reluctance. Is it doubt, fear of being selfish, or a belief that it's unattainable? As you think about this, consider what steps you can take to begin to include these larger requests in your prayers, thus fostering a deeper trust in the limitless possibilities of prayer.

As you explore the following questions, you will delve deeper into your fears and open the door to a more fulfilling and daring prayer life. Let these reflections guide you as you break down the barriers of fear, step into a space of bold faith, and embrace the vast potential of your prayers.

Take Action

Moving from contemplation to action is critical to overcoming the fear of asking for monumental things. The path may seem challenging, but remember that every significant accomplishment begins with the courage to take the first step. Identify a "big thing" that you have hesitated to pray for-a longing for personal growth, a change in your community, or a deep-seated dream that you have held back from pursuing out of fear. This first step is a leap toward empowerment and self-discovery that promises a future of growth and fulfillment.

With this "big thing" in mind, cultivate a mindset of boldness and faith. Ground your desires in the belief that what you are asking for has the potential to align with a greater purpose. Prepare your heart by reflecting on the stories of bold prayer in this book, understanding that these stories prove what is possible when faith is put into action.

Let these stories inspire and encourage you on your journey of faith and prayer.

Next, commit your prayer to writing. Writing down your thoughts and desires makes your prayer tangible and serves as a constant reminder of your faith. As you write, you outline your request and strengthen your belief in the possibility of its fulfillment - an exercise in clarity and faith.

Then make it a habit to pray boldly and consistently. Prayer is not a one-time event, but an ongoing conversation with God.[8] Let your prayers for this "big thing" be frequent, passionate, and full of anticipation. Embrace the perseverance of Hannah and the unwavering faith of Rosa Parks. Be open to the possibility of waiting, understanding that patience is crucial to receiving. This waiting is not a time of uncertainty, but a peaceful assurance that your prayer will be heard and answered in the best way and at the right time.

Finally, be open to taking practical steps in your prayer. Faith and action go together. As you pray boldly, ask for guidance on the actions you need to take. Sometimes accomplishing monumental things requires effort - acquiring new skills, forging new relationships, or putting ourselves in positions where our prayers can be manifested. In this way, your prayer becomes a living, breathing entity that brings you closer to the breakthrough you seek with each step.

---

[8] Resisting Temptation: Mastering The Art of Overcoming With The Power Of Prayer » THE CATHOLIC.
https://thecatholic.online/how-to-beat-the-temptation-with-prayer/

Identify a specific area where you have been afraid to ask God for something important-a personal goal, dream, or challenge. Spend time reflecting on the roots of this fear and ask God to help you overcome it. Once you have identified it, make a commitment to pray regularly and consistently for this "big thing. Write it down and seek the support and guidance of other believers as you pray.

Remember to trust in God's power and promises, and expect great things as you pray with confidence. Use specific scriptures or promises as the basis for your requests. Ask God to help you overcome your fear and give you the faith and courage to ask for the monumental things that matter most.

By taking these steps, you are embarking on a transformational journey where prayer goes beyond mere words and becomes a channel for profound change. Let your boldness be rooted in the conviction that your deepest desires, when brought humbly before the throne, have the power to reshape realities and align them with a greater divine purpose.

Chapter 3:
How To Pray With Confidence and Expectation

Acknowledging the power of prayer is central to this journey toward spiritual strength and renewal. Praying with confidence and expectation isn't just about believing that something good might happen; it's about trusting wholeheartedly that our prayers will be heard and answered, even if the answers come in unexpected forms. This chapter explores the transformative nature of such prayer.

Confidence in prayer begins with understanding who we are talking to. We're not just throwing words into the void or wishing for stars. We're communicating with the Creator of the universe who knows us intimately and desires a relationship with us. This fundamental truth changes everything about how we approach prayer.

Expectation, on the other hand, is about holding a space in our hearts for God's response. It's about believing that something will happen when we pray. It doesn't mean we dictate outcomes or timelines to God; instead, we prepare ourselves to receive, fully trusting that God's plans for us are filled with hope and purpose.

Elijah's experience on Mount Carmel is a powerful example of confident and expectant prayer. He didn't just hope that God would answer; he prepared for the answer before it came. This attitude shows a deep trust in God's promise and power, an attitude we should emulate.

Martin Luther King Jr.'s prayers during the civil rights movement exemplify this courageous approach. He prayed for the strength to endure and for victory over injustice, fully expecting God to move mountains in his time. His prayers were infused with a vision of what was right and an unwavering faith in God's ability to bring about change.

To pray with confidence, we must first align our hearts with God's. This includes spending time in His Word, understanding His character, and recognizing His sovereignty over all things. The more we know about God, the more confident we will grow in Him.

But knowing God isn't just an intellectual exercise; it's about building relationships. As in any relationship, communication is essential. Prayer is how we talk to God; through the Bible, God talks to us. This two-way conversation strengthens our connection and builds our confidence in His care for us.

Expectation requires humility. It's an acknowledgment that while we may have desires and requests, God's will ultimately prevails. Expectant prayer submits to this divine wisdom, trusting that whether God's answers are "yes," "no," or "wait," they are always in our best interest.

Including thanksgiving in our prayers also builds confidence and expectation. We remind ourselves of His faithfulness by remembering and thanking God for past answered prayers and blessings. This creates a cycle of trust and gratitude that strengthens our prayer life.

Another critical aspect is perseverance. Praying with confidence and expectation means being persistent, like the widow in Jesus' parable who kept coming to the judge for justice. Our persistence demonstrates our faith and trust in God's perfect timing and answer.

Praying together with others can also strengthen our confidence and expectations. There's power in prayer together-when two or three gather in His name, there is a unique promise of His presence. Sharing our prayers and witnessing the prayers of others builds our faith and encourages us to believe in more extraordinary things.

Visualizing our prayers being answered can also be a powerful expectation-building exercise. This doesn't mean that we get lost in wishful thinking, but that we actively imagine and believe in the positive changes we pray for, aligning our minds and hearts with God's promises.

Finally, an attitude of readiness is crucial. Praying with confidence and expectation means preparing to step out in faith when God provides an answer. Sometimes the answer to our prayers requires us to take action, make a move, or embrace change.

When we cultivate these attitudes and practices, our prayers are transformed from mere words into deep conversations with God, filled with confidence and expectation. Let's embark on this journey of bold prayer, asking boldly, trusting implicitly, and receiving graciously, knowing that our prayers are powerful and effective not because of who we are, but because of who God is.

In conclusion, praying with confidence and expectation is not just a technique; it's a way of life. It changes our perceptions, strengthens our faith, and deepens our relationship with God. When we embrace this approach, we become beacons of hope and faith, witnessing to God's unfailing love and power in our lives.

Elijah Prayed With Confidence and Expectation

Imagine standing alone on a mountaintop, the weight of a nation's spiritual betrayal on your shoulders, ready to challenge the prophets of Baal in a dramatic display of faith versus idolatry. This was Elijah's reality - a moment that would forever be remembered as a turning point in Israel's history. Elijah's prayer at this critical moment didn't just echo through the valleys of Mount Carmel; it has echoed through the ages as a testament to the power of praying with confidence and expectation.

Elijah's story is not just a narrative from ancient texts, but a living template for our prayer life today. When he stepped forward to pray for God's fire to consume the sacrifice on Mount Carmel, his prayer was concise, powerful, and filled with an unwavering confidence in God's ability to respond. Elijah didn't shout or dance; his confidence was not in the volume of his request, but in the One to whom he was praying.

What distinguished Elijah was his unwavering expectation of God's action. He didn't pray wondering if God would respond; he prayed knowing that God would. This expectation wasn't born of naiveté; it was rooted in his intimate relationship with God. He knew God's character- that He is faithful, just, and responsive to the cries of His people.

To pray like Elijah is to understand the God to whom we pray. It requires a deep relationship, a recognition of God's sovereignty, and an unyielding faith in His power. We must know His promises and His precedent of faithfulness in Scripture and in our lives, and let these truths shape our prayers into declarations of faith, not just petitions of hope.

Praying with confidence and expectation doesn't guarantee a "yes" to every request. Elijah's effectiveness in prayer came not from getting what he wanted, but from seeking what God wanted. His confidence was more in God's wisdom to choose the right outcome than in his desires. This perspective changes the way we pray, moving us from a demanding attitude to submission to God's will.

In our discussions of courageous prayer, it's important to distinguish confidence in what we ask from confidence in who we ask. Our confidence is not in the power of our prayers or the details of our requests, but in the power and wisdom of God to do exceedingly abundantly beyond all that we ask or think.

Moreover, expectation in prayer is not passive; it's not wishful thinking. Instead, it's an active, living hope. After praying, Elijah sent his servant to look for signs of rain seven times, vividly demonstrating his determination. He acted on his faith, fully expecting God's answer. Like Elijah, our prayers should move us to expectant action, seeking and working for the fulfillment of our prayers.

The life of Elijah encourages us to step out of the shadows of hesitation into the bold light of confident prayer. This step may feel unfamiliar or even uncomfortable at first. But as we understand and experience God's character, our prayers will naturally become more confident and expectant.

Elijah's account on Mount Carmel refutes the notion that only the "spiritual elite" can pray boldly. Elijah was a man "with a nature like ours" (James 5:17), yet his prayer opened the heavens to fire and rain. This invites us to see the potential in our prayers, regardless of our status or spiritual pedigree.

In times of challenge and decision, we should trust in God's steadfastness, not the severity of our circumstances. We must stand in faith like Elijah, even when we face seemingly insurmountable odds.

Embodying confidence and expectation in our prayers also means preparing for God's timing. We often pray expecting an immediate response, forgetting that God's timing is perfect. Elijah understood this and waited patiently and persistently for God's intervention. Our prayers, too, should be characterized by perseverance and trust in God's perfect timing.

We must also recognize the power of praying in accordance with God's will. Elijah's confidence came from his alignment with God's desire to reveal Himself to Israel. When we seek God's will in prayer, aligning our desires with His, we pray with the authority that comes from seeking not our own agenda, but God's.

We must build our relationship with God to cultivate a prayer life of confidence and expectation. Knowing Him-His character, His promises, and His faithfulness-gives us the confidence to pray bold prayers. Spend time in Scripture, abide in His presence, and allow your prayers to reflect your growing understanding of God.

Finally, let's remember that confidence and expectation in prayer are not just for our walk with God. They're tools for intercession, for standing in the gap for others, just as Elijah did for Israel. As you grow in praying with confidence and expectation, let your prayers go beyond your needs and reach out in bold faith for the transformation of the world around you.

Elijah's story is a powerful reminder that prayer, when offered with confidence and expectation, can transform not only individual hearts but entire nations. As we learn to pray in this way, may we see the fruit of such prayers in our lives, our communities, and our world.

Martin Luther King Prayed With Confidence And Expectation

Certain figures stand tall in the annals of history, not only for their actions, but also for the depth of their faith and the strength of their convictions. Martin Luther King, Jr. is one such figure whose prayers weren't just a ritual, but a profound dialogue with the Divine. His prayer life was marked by an unwavering confidence and an anticipation of great breakthroughs, setting a compelling example for anyone seeking to deepen their prayer practice.[9]

King's approach to prayer was grounded in the belief that it was essential to sustaining his spirit in the midst of the trials and tribulations of the civil rights movement. He understood prayer as more than just seeking divine intervention; it was about aligning his purpose with God's, thereby equipping himself with the spiritual armor necessary for the battles he faced. This alignment didn't happen alone in silence or solitude, but often in the

---

[9] TB. *Martin Luther King – Prayer Was His Secret | Sisters of St. Francis of Sylvania, Ohio.* sistersosf.org/our-legacy-lives-on-pilgrimages-for-franciscan-leadership-2/.

[9] "Prayers" | The Martin Luther King, Jr. Research and Education Institute." *Kinginstitute.stanford.edu*, kinginstitute.stanford.edu/king-papers/documents/prayers.

company of others, underscoring the communal aspect of prayer that was central to King's ethos.[10]

When King prayed, he did so with the expectation that God would listen and act. Such expectation comes from a place of deep faith, where the certainty of God's promises overshadows doubt. In his famous "I Have a Dream" speech, the cadence of a pastor's prayer echoes, offering the world a glimpse into the soul of a man who communicated with the divine as naturally as he did with his fellow man.

King's confidence in prayer was not misplaced optimism, but was based on a fundamental understanding of biblical promises. He drew on scriptures that affirmed the power of faith and the assurance that those who seek shall find. For King, this was not just theory; it was a lived experience. He faced significant challenges, but he achieved incredible victories both personally and in the broader civil rights movement by praying for guidance, strength, and justice.

To pray like Martin Luther King is to pray with a heart full of faith, eyes set on what can be, and hands ready to work to make that vision a reality. It's important to understand that prayer is not a passive act, but an active engagement with the divine, a co-creation of the world as it should be, rooted in love, justice, and equality.

A critical takeaway from King's prayer life is the need for greater separation between his spiritual practice and his activism. His prayer was integrated into every aspect of his life, fueling his passion for justice and his unwavering belief in nonviolent resistance. This holistic approach to prayer is something everyone can incorporate into their lives, bridging the gap between spiritual belief and daily action.

King's expectation of God's response was not vague or undefined. He prayed with specific results in mind, whether it was the success of the Montgomery bus boycott, the passage of civil rights legislation, or the safety of those marching with him. This specificity in prayer is a model for personal petition, emphasizing the importance of clarity and faith in asking for what one needs or desires.

King's prayers were not only for change, but also for him to be an instrument of the change he sought. This proactive attitude toward prayer is crucial for anyone who wants to make a difference in their lives or in the world around them.

Another characteristic of King's prayer was its rootedness in community. He often spoke of the interconnectedness of all people, regardless of race, religion, or nationality. His prayers reflected this belief, seeking individual or group victories and the uplift and liberation of all oppressed peoples. This communal focus reminds us that our prayers can and should reach beyond our immediate concerns to a more universal perspective.

King also understood the importance of perseverance in prayer. He faced numerous setbacks in his fight for civil rights, yet he remained steadfast in his faith and commitment to prayer. This persistence is a lesson in the power of resilience, teaching us that answers to prayer may not always come in the form we expect or as quickly as we hope, but that does not mean our prayers are unheard.

In times of despair or in the face of seemingly insurmountable obstacles, embracing King's approach to prayer can serve as a beacon of hope. It offers a path to personal peace and to creating ripples of change that can transform the world.

To embody the essence of Martin Luther King's approach to prayer, we should view each prayer as a seed of change, planted with hope, watered with faith, and expected to blossom into actions that reflect our deepest convictions. We should pray with a heart open to the transforming power of the divine and a commitment to be part of that transformation.

In conclusion, Martin Luther King's prayer life is a powerful testament to the potential of faith in action. His example challenges us to elevate our prayers from mere words to a dynamic force for personal growth and social change. Praying with confidence and expectation, as King did, opens us up to receiving divine blessings and becoming vessels through which those blessings can flow into the world.

As we continue our spiritual journeys, let us be inspired by the legacy of Martin Luther King. May his approach to prayer invigorate our faith, amplify our actions, and deepen our commitment to a world where justice, love, and peace are not just ideals but lived realities.

Chapter Three Discussion Questions

After exploring Praying with Confidence and Expectation, it is important to delve deeper into personal reflection and understanding. These questions will help you assess your prayer life, identify areas for growth, and inspire you to pray with boldness and expectation. Let's dive in.

1. **Reflect on Your Current Level of Confidence in Prayer:** On a scale of 1-10, how confident do you feel when you pray? Consider what factors might contribute to your current level of confidence. Is it your understanding of God, past experiences with

prayer, or doubts about what you are asking for? How can you address these factors to increase your confidence in prayer?

2. **Identify Your Expectations:** What do you expect to happen when you pray? Are your expectations more hopeful or tentative? Discuss the implications of having a positive expectation when you pray and how cultivating a mindset of expectation can transform your prayer life. Reflect on the stories of Elijah and Martin Luther King Jr. presented in this chapter. How did their expectations affect their confidence and their results?

3. **Challenges to Praying Boldly:** Bold prayer often comes with challenges, including fear of disappointment or feeling unworthy to ask for big things. Identify and share personal challenges you've faced in praying boldly. How have these challenges impacted your prayer life? Discuss strategies for overcoming these barriers so that you can pray more confidently and expectantly.

Addressing these questions is just the beginning. As you consider your answers, allow yourself to be open to change and growth. Prayer is a powerful tool for transformation- not just in your circumstances, but in your heart and mind. Embrace this journey of discovery and let your prayers reflect your bold faith and bright hope for the future.

Take Action

After exploring the importance of praying with confidence and expectation, it is important to put it into practice. You've encountered the stories of Elijah and Martin Luther

King, who stood as figures of faith and embodiments of spiritual audacity. Their stories illuminate not the path of the timid, but the path for those who dare to harness the divine in their daily walk. Now it's your turn.

Begin this transformative journey by setting aside a specific time each day for prayer alone.[11] This isn't about routine, but about creating a sacred space for dialog with the Divine. During this time, let your prayers reflect the conviction and anticipation that characterized those who've gone boldly before us. Speak as if what you're asking for is already on its way to you, for faith is the currency that moves mountains in the realm of faith.

Next, incorporate journaling into your prayer routine. Document not only your requests, but also the progress of your faith journey. This will serve as both a testament to your spiritual growth and a practical way to track the unfolding answers to your prayers. Witnessing the tangible manifestations of your petitions will not only strengthen your faith, but also serve as a beacon of encouragement in moments of doubt.

Furthermore, prayer should not be a monologue, but a dialogue. Include silence in your practice, allowing space for response, sensation, and intuition. Clarity often comes in these quiet moments, and you may find the direction or certainty you've been seeking. Remember that expectation in prayer is not only about anticipating answers, but also about being open to guidance in forms you may not have imagined.

---

[11] Praying Continually (2024). https://thewitness.org/praying-continually/

In conclusion, embarking on a path of confident and expectant prayer is a journey of becoming. It shapes your spiritual life and forms you into a vessel capable of receiving, recognizing and responding to the Divine. Your actions today are the seeds of the miracles you'll harvest tomorrow. So step forward with courage, clothe yourself in expectation, and watch as your prayer life transforms your inner landscape and outer reality.

Chapter 4:
Pray For Bold Breakthroughs
In Your Finances

Trying to manage our finances can sometimes feel like wandering through a vast and confusing wilderness. It is easy to become discouraged in the face of seemingly endless obstacles. Yet it is precisely in this challenge that we find a powerful opportunity for growth and transformation. This chapter dives into the realm of financial breakthroughs, not through conventional methods, but through the powerful tool of prayer. The stories of Job and Frederick Douglass provide profound insights into the journey to financial empowerment through faith and intentional prayer.

Financial breakthrough is not simply an increase in wealth. It involves a holistic transformation in how we perceive, interact with, and manage our resources. Faith, especially bold prayer, plays a critical role in this transformation. It's about recognizing that our financial situations, no matter how dire, can be miraculously transformed when we align our desires with God's will.

Consider Job, a man of immense faith who faced unprecedented loss, including wealth. Yet his story is not just one of loss, but of restoration and abundance through unwavering faith. Job's breakthrough prayer wasn't just a request for the restoration of wealth. Instead, it was a profound submission to God's will and an understanding of God's sovereignty over all aspects of life, including finances. His journey teaches us that breakthroughs often follow profound trials, and our response to those trials can determine the outcome.

Similarly, Frederick Douglass, while not a biblical figure, exemplifies the power of bold prayer to overcome seemingly insurmountable financial and personal obstacles. Born into slavery, Douglass' journey to freedom was fraught with peril. Yet his unwavering faith and bold prayers led to his physical freedom and financial empowerment as a free man. His life is a testament to the power of faith to shape our destiny, including our financial well-being.

But how do we pray for financial breakthroughs? It begins with faith-faith not in the power of our desires, but in the omnipotence and goodness of the Divine. It's about recognizing that while we play a role in managing our resources, the ultimate source of all provision is God.

Next, we must pray with specificity. It's not enough to ask for "financial blessings. What is your need? Is it a debt that you're struggling with? Is it a job you've been praying for? Or wisdom to better manage your finances? Specify it in your prayers. This level of specificity not only clarifies your needs, but also strengthens your faith as you place your precise requests before God.

It is important to take action along with bold prayers for financial breakthroughs. According to Scripture, faith without works is dead. This means being diligent in seeking opportunities, wise in financial management, and generous in giving. Our actions are a testament to our faith, a tangible expression of our trust in God's provision.[12]

Praying for bold financial breakthroughs also involves surrender-a concept that may seem counterintuitive in a society that often equates financial success with control. But surrender here does not mean passivity. Rather, it means acknowledging our limitations and entrusting our financial concerns and aspirations to a power higher than ourselves. It declares our dependence on divine grace for provision and guidance.

Patience is essential on this journey. Immediate answers to prayer are only sometimes the norm; sometimes the answer is different from what we expect. Yet within this waiting lies a powerful opportunity for spiritual growth that deepens our trust in divine timing and wisdom.

In addition, our prayers for financial breakthrough must be infused with gratitude. Gratitude shifts our focus from what we lack to the blessings we have, however small they may seem.[13] This doesn't deny the realities of our financial struggles but helps cultivate a mindset of abundance, which is crucial to attracting more blessings.

It is also crucial to pray against any obstacles that block our financial breakthrough. These can be internal, such as fear and doubt, or external, such as systemic injustices. Our prayers should be bold in asking for these obstacles to be

---

[12] Tithes and Offering (Scripture Verses, Prayer, & Full Explanation). https://www.dailyeffectiveprayer.org/tithes-and-offering/

[13] Prayer: The Antidote to an Anxious Heart | Alex Nazarene. https://alexnazarene.org/2023/09/06/prayer-the-antidote-to-an-anxious-heart/

removed, trusting in God's power to make a way where there seems to be none.

Job's story didn't end in despair; it ended with twice what had been taken from him. Douglass didn't remain enslaved; he became a pivotal figure in the abolitionist movement, using his financial resources for the greater good. Their stories remind us of the transforming power of faith and prayer in our financial lives.

As we close this chapter, remember that every financial challenge is an opportunity for spiritual breakthrough. We open ourselves to divine intervention when we approach our financial dilemmas with bold prayers rooted in faith, specificity, action, surrender, patience, gratitude, and a prayerful rebuke of obstacles.

We are committed to financial abundance and a life that reflects the richness of God's purpose. Let your financial journey be a testament to the power of bold prayer. Embark on this journey with the assurance that divine providence can turn scarcity into abundance, ruin into renewal.

In the next chapter, we will look at praying boldly for your marriage and family, another critical area of our lives that requires divine wisdom, guidance, and provision.

Job's Breakthrough Prayer

In our quest for spiritual and financial breakthroughs, few stories resonate as deeply as that of Job. Job stood firm, his faith unwavering in the face of dire circumstances, setting an example that transcends time. It's not just the determination in the face of adversity, but his deep trust in the divine that we seek to emulate. This chapter delves into the essence of Job's breakthrough prayer, illustrating how his resilient faith underscores our attempts to seek bold financial breakthroughs through worship.

First, Job's story exemplifies unjust suffering. Here was a man who had lost everything-wealth, family, and health. Yet his response to these calamities wasn't one of despair, but rather an appeal to God's fairness and justice. Through his discourse, Job's prayers move from questioning to submission, highlighting a crucial lesson-the importance of reaffirming our commitment to God, especially in the face of financial devastation.

Job's breakthrough prayer isn't a miracle formula; rather, his attitude of humility and steadfast faith sets the stage for divine intervention. Despite his righteous life, Job recognized that God's wisdom and plans were beyond his understanding. This humility is critical as we pray for financial breakthroughs. Recognizing that our efforts are secondary to God's grace is essential to cultivating a heart that is receptive to God's will.

In addition, Job's dialogues with God reveal a boldness that comes from an intimate relationship with the divine. He wasn't afraid to state his case before God, showing us the importance of being open in our prayers. It's important to share our deepest desires and fears with God, including those regarding our finances, with the assurance that He will listen.

One of the most profound elements of Job's prayer life was his perseverance. Despite God's prolonged silence and the discouraging advice of his friends, Job remained steadfast in his faith. This perseverance is critical in our prayers for financial breakthroughs. The journey may be fraught with setbacks, but our continued commitment to worship is an act of faith that signals our trust in God's timing and provision.

The eventual restoration of Job's fortunes wasn't just a reversal of fortune, but a testament to the power of persistent prayer and unyielding faith. The story culminates in a demonstration of God's goodness and sovereignty, assuring us that divine restoration often surpasses our original condition. When we pray for financial breakthroughs, it's with the expectation of not just recovery, but abundance, in keeping with God's generosity.

It is critical to understand the central message of Job's prayer. It was not about material possessions or wealth, but about a deep understanding and trust in God. Our prayers for financial breakthroughs should similarly come from a desire to align ourselves more closely with God's will and to use every blessing given to His glory.

The story of Job reminds us that God's presence is not based solely on financial blessings. Despite losing everything, his faith remained steadfast. This challenges us to evaluate our own motivations for seeking financial breakthroughs and encourages us to find contentment and trust in God's plans regardless of our current financial situation.

Engaging in Job's breakthrough prayer requires reflection. It's an opportunity to assess the depth of our faith and the alignment of our financial desires with our spiritual values. Do we seek God's hand more than His face? Such introspection is essential to forging a prayer life that seeks financial blessings and closer communion with the divine.

In addition, Job's experience invites us to embrace community and support in our prayer journey. Just as Job's friends eventually came to a deeper understanding and support of his situation, so too should we seek and offer such fellowship. Sharing our financial struggles within a community of faith can strengthen our spirits and multiply the power of our prayers.

Integrating Job's approach into our prayers for financial breakthrough involves embracing humility, cultivating intimacy with God, persevering despite silence or setbacks, and prioritizing spiritual direction over material gain. It's a holistic approach that nourishes our faith as we navigate the complexities of financial challenges.

As we reflect on Job's breakthrough prayer, let's approach our financial requests with a new perspective. Embarking on a journey of faith draws us closer to God's heart, not just the provision of resources. Our prayers of humility, honesty, and trust can lead to breakthroughs that are both spiritual and financial.

In conclusion, the story of Job offers an illuminating path for those seeking financial breakthroughs through prayer. It's a story that encourages resilience, demands faithfulness, and promises restoration. As we incorporate these principles into our prayer lives, let us remain confident that God is willing and able to transform our financial desolation into abundance that enhances our spiritual growth and reflects His glory.

Therefore, as we move forward, let this chapter on Job's breakthrough prayer serve as a beacon to guide us through our financial trials with unwavering faith and boldness. It's a testament to the power of prayer, reminding us that breakthroughs are possible and assured when we seek God earnestly, with humility and perseverance.

Fredrick Douglass's Breakthrough Prayer

At the heart of every significant transformation lies a spark of courage that ignites the desire for change. In the journey toward financial breakthrough, that spark often manifests itself through prayer. Among the most powerful examples of such transformative prayer is that of Frederick Douglass, an icon of resilience and faith in the face of seemingly insurmountable challenges. His story illustrates the power of bold prayer and serves as a beacon of hope for anyone seeking a breakthrough in their financial circumstances.

From an early age, Frederick Douglass knew the sting of poverty and the bondage of slavery. Yet he harbored a vision for a life far beyond the cotton fields and cruel bondage that defined his early years. His prayers were not just for personal gain, but included a broader hope for freedom and prosperity for all who suffered under the yoke of slavery. Through his strong faith, Douglass recognized that financial freedom was inextricably linked to spiritual and physical liberation.

What distinguishes Frederick Douglass's prayers is their audacity. He prayed not only for survival, but also for prosperity, the opportunity to use his talents to their fullest potential, and the wisdom to manage his resources wisely once he had achieved it. This was a man who, in the midst of bondage, dared to pray not only for deliverance, but for a future in which he could contribute to the economic fabric of the country.

His groundbreaking prayer, whispered in the dead of night and echoed across the fields, was a testament to his unyielding faith in a future he had yet to see. It was a prayer that transcended personal desires and sought a collective breakthrough for his people. Frederick Douglass understood that true financial breakthroughs come when we align our prayers with a vision that transcends our immediate needs and includes the well-being of others.

This concept is critical for anyone praying for financial breakthroughs today. It challenges us to broaden our perspective and pray with a heart for the greater good. Frederick Douglass' story challenges us to reflect on our intentions and ask if our prayers include the welfare of those around us. It forces us to consider whether we are praying only for our success or for the flourishing of all.

Another lesson from the life of Frederick Douglass is the importance of action. Prayer was critical, but his relentless pursuit of freedom, his thirst for knowledge, and his unwavering commitment to justice catalyzed his breakthroughs. Prayer is essential, but it must be coupled with action to achieve financial deliverance. One must work hard to achieve breakthroughs.

For Frederick Douglass, breakthrough prayer also meant confronting the systems of oppression that held him and others in bondage. This means recognizing and challenging the structures that perpetuate economic inequality today. Praying for financial breakthroughs thus becomes an act of defiance against injustice, a call for divine intervention in our lives, and a means of transforming the societal constructs that hinder economic mobility for many.

The power of Frederick Douglass's breakthrough prayer lies in its boldness, its expansive vision, and its foundation in deep faith. It teaches us that we shouldn't aim small when we pray for financial breakthroughs. Bold prayers have the power to transform individual circumstances and change the course of history. Douglass's life is a testament to the monumental impact that such prayer, action, and a heart for justice can have.

Like Frederick Douglass, our prayers for financial breakthroughs should be infused with hope, resilience, and a vision beyond personal gain. They should seek wisdom for wealth creation, resource stewardship, and inclusive prosperity that uplifts communities.

In addition, the story of Frederick Douglass encourages us to keep hope alive, even when our financial breakthroughs seem distant. His journey from slavery to becoming a leading voice for abolition and civil rights underscores that the most unlikely breakthroughs are within reach with faith and perseverance.

By embracing the essence of Frederick Douglass' breakthrough prayer, we are called to adopt a mindset that views financial challenges not as insurmountable obstacles, but as opportunities for growth and transformation. It's a mindset that recognizes the power of prayer to transform our financial situation and inspire lives of purpose, generosity and impact.

Ultimately, Frederick Douglass' life and prayers remind us that financial breakthroughs are not just about achieving wealth. It's about achieving a form of freedom that allows us to realize our full potential, contribute to the well-being of others, and advance the cause of justice in the world. His legacy challenges us to imagine and pray for personal and expansive community wealth.

As we seek our breakthroughs, let us be inspired by Frederick Douglass. Let us pray boldly, act with conviction, and maintain an unwavering faith to overcome obstacles. Remember that our prayers for financial prosperity should also be prayers for freedom, justice, and a better world.

In the spirit of Frederick Douglass' breakthrough prayer, may we too experience the profound transformation that comes when faith, vision and action come together. And may our bold prayers for financial breakthroughs not only transform our lives, but also contribute to the unfolding of a more just and prosperous world for future generations.

Chapter Four Discussion Questions

As we explore the importance of praying for bold breakthroughs in our finances, it's important to absorb the stories and lessons presented and actively engage with the material through introspective and thought-provoking questions. The questions below encourage you to think deeply about your financial situation, your relationship with money, and how your faith intersects with these areas. Let's explore:

1. **Reflect on Job's and Frederick Douglass's prayers for financial breakthrough.** Consider their circumstances, their faith, and the boldness of their requests. How does their approach to prayer in times of financial need inspire you to pray differently about your financial challenges?

2. **Examine your own beliefs and attitudes towards money.** Examine your own beliefs and attitudes about money. How do you think your faith and prayer life affect your current financial situation? Are there areas in your financial life where you've struggled to pray

boldly for breakthroughs? What is holding you back?

3. **Consider the role of faith in financial stewardship.** Given what you've learned, how can you incorporate bold prayers into your financial planning and stewardship? Think about practical steps you can take to align your financial goals with your faith, ensuring that you're not just seeking abundance for its own sake but for its potential to positively impact the kingdom.

These questions are intended to provoke thought and inspire action. As you ponder them, remember that the journey to financial breakthrough is not just about reciting perfect prayers. It's about developing a deeper trust in God's provision and timing. Allow these discussions to fuel your personal reflections and conversations with fellow believers. Let's support each other by praying boldly for breakthrough in every area of our lives.

Take Action

Now that we've explored the transformative power of bold prayer in our financial lives through the examples of Job and Frederick Douglass, it's time to put this knowledge into action. Prayer is not passive; it requires participation, faith, and sometimes a push out of our comfort zone. Our finances often reflect our inner beliefs and fears. Therefore, taking bold steps in prayer can be the catalyst for spiritual and material breakthroughs.

Let's start with clarity. Clearly articulate what financial breakthrough means to you. Is it freedom from debt? A new job? Giving more generously? Write down your specific financial goals. This act of writing is a physical manifestation of your faith, a step toward making your prayers tangible. Remember, clarity in your intentions paves the way for focused prayers that can cut through the chaos of our lives to bring about change.

Next, commit to a daily time of prayer focused solely on your finances. This doesn't mean that you will only pray about money, but it does mean that you are committed to seeing change in this area through the power of prayer. In these moments, use the stories of Job and Douglass as inspiration. They faced monumental challenges, yet they remained steadfast in their faith. Their stories remind us that no matter the size of our financial obstacles, our determination in prayer can lead to breakthroughs.

In addition, engage in acts of faith that match your prayers. If you're praying for a new job, start applying. If you're praying for freedom from debt, create a budget or debt reduction plan. Action is the proof of your faith, the physical counterpart to your spiritual efforts. Through these actions and bold prayers, you're telling yourself and the Divine that you're serious about seeing change in your finances.

Finally, surround yourself with a community of faith. Share your prayers for financial breakthrough with friends, family, or a prayer group that can support you on this journey. This network can offer encouragement, hold you accountable, and pray with you. Remember, shared faith and collective prayer are powerful forces that can amplify your requests and lead to corporate and personal victories.

In essence, taking bold steps in prayer for your financial life is about clarity, commitment, action, and community. It's a holistic approach that combines the spiritual and the practical, leading to transformative breakthroughs. Let's embark on this journey with faith, knowing that our bold prayers can and will usher in a new era of financial freedom and abundance.

Chapter 5: Praying Boldly for Your Marriage and Family

Few areas of the faith journey touch the core of our lives as deeply as our marriages and families. In these intimate relationships, we see the potential for deep joy and sometimes deep pain. Embracing the power of courageous prayer for our loved ones can lead to transformational experiences that reverberate throughout our homes.

Focusing first on marriage, it's important to understand that bold prayer is not about asking for specific results. Instead, it's about inviting divine guidance and power into the relationship. It's about seeking wisdom beyond our understanding in order to foster a bond that can withstand life's inevitable challenges. For example, when we pray for patience or empathy in our interactions with our spouse, we are asking for temporary peace and rooted growth that enhances our connection.

Praying boldly is critical to navigating family dynamics in today's world of outside influences. Praying boldly for our children means asking for a shield of protection over their minds and hearts. It's seeking wisdom for ourselves to guide them in a way that is consistent with enduring values, even when societal trends push in the opposite direction.

So how do you pray boldly for your marriage and family? Start with transparency. Approach these prayer sessions with an open heart, sharing your fears, hopes, and desires without reservation. In these moments of vulnerability, prayer transforms from routine to deep dialogue.

Next, embrace gratitude. Making it a habit to thank the Divine for your spouse, children, and blessings, no matter how small, cultivates an environment of positivity that strengthens family bonds. Remember, it's not about ignoring challenges; it's about recognizing the good in the midst of the trials.

In addition, specificity in your prayers can make a noticeable difference. Instead of general requests for happiness or well-being, get down to the details. Pray for your spouse's job challenges, your child's school project, or a family member's health concern. It's these specific prayers that often bring tangible evidence of their power.

An essential aspect of praying boldly is persistence. There will be moments when you feel like your prayers are hitting the ceiling, but remember that transformation often happens below the surface, unseen until it blooms. The biblical story of Daniel shows us the impact of unyielding faith and prayer; even though he faced lions, his persistent prayer and faithfulness protected him.

Include prayers for emotional wisdom and physical health. A family that prays for spiritual clarity and emotional intelligence tends to handle conflict more constructively. Praying for health doesn't guarantee immunity from disease, but it creates a spiritual bulwark that often leads to better physical stewardship.

To deepen the effect, make this a communal activity. Praying with your spouse and children strengthens your faith and brings your hearts closer together. It's a powerful witness to the younger generation about the role of religion in overcoming life's hurdles.

In addition, include Bible stories and promises in your prayers. The stories of Abraham's faith, Hannah's perseverance, and Job's perseverance provide rich ground for inspiration. These stories remind us that we are part of a larger, ongoing story of faith.

It's also important to listen carefully during and after these times of prayer. Often the answers come in quiet whispers through daily events or the words of others. Keep your heart and ears open to discern these answers.

Finally, remember to celebrate the victories, both large and small. Acknowledging answered prayers fosters an attitude of expectation and faith that encourages further prayer. Celebrations can be simple, from a meal together to verbal acknowledgement during family gatherings.

In conclusion, praying boldly for your marriage and family transforms the present circumstances and the legacy you leave behind. It's about anchoring your loved ones in a faith that can withstand life's storms. As you embark on this journey, remember that bold prayer can lead to remarkable changes in the heart of your family.

Let this chapter serve as a starting point for cultivating a vibrant, prayer-centered home. It's a path that promises spiritual growth and a deeper connection with your loved ones. As we've seen through countless stories, boldly lifting up our marriages and families in prayer is undoubtedly a profound catalyst for renewal and joy.

The journey may seem daunting at times, but the rewards reflected in the lives of those who've walked this path are boundless. With each prayer, you step into the potential of what your family can become when rooted in faith, love, and bold prayer. It's a transformation that not only transforms your home, but leaves a lasting impact on future generations.

Priscilla and Aquila Prays Boldly

The foundational element of bold prayer lies at the heart of every thriving marriage and family. To grasp this importance, we turn to the commendable example of Priscilla and Aquila, a couple whose story offers profound insights into the power of unified, faith-filled petitions to God. Their journey illustrates the power of mutual support and the remarkable results of two hearts united in seeking divine intervention for their relationship and home.

Priscilla and Aquila were not mere bystanders in the early Christian community; they were active participants, fervently contributing to the fabric of their spiritual family through teaching and hospitality. But what set them apart was their commitment to pray boldly together, not just for their own needs, but for the advancement of God's kingdom. This shared spiritual discipline forged an unbreakable bond and demonstrated the transformative power of united prayer in marriage.

What does it mean to pray boldly for your marriage and family in the manner of Priscilla and Aquila? It means having the audacity to ask for more than the absence of conflict or the provision of daily needs. It's about seeking deep spiritual awakening in your relationship, divine guidance in your decisions, and blessings that extend beyond your immediate environment to impact your community.

Consider the impact of their prayers in the early church, creating an environment ripe for miracles, teaching, and growth. Their approach to prayer wasn't casual or reserved;

they understood the weight of their words and the power of their God to effect change. This isn't just a call to action; it's an invitation to experience a deeper, more fulfilling connection with your spouse and with God.

To begin this journey, it's crucial to cultivate an expectation that God not only hears, but delights in answering the bold prayers you and your spouse bring before Him. The story of Priscilla and Aquila teaches us that there's no limit to what can be accomplished when faith is shared and expressed together in prayer.

Praying boldly also involves vulnerability-to your partner and to God. It's about opening up your deepest hopes, fears, and desires, believing that transparency in prayer leads to spiritual intimacy and mutual growth. When you surrender everything to God, your relationship is strengthened, your faith is deepened, and your family becomes a beacon of God's love.

Another critical aspect learned from Priscilla and Aquila is the importance of being intentional. Set aside dedicated time for prayer together, free from distractions, and make this practice a non-negotiable part of your daily routine. This consistent, intentional approach to prayer builds a solid foundation for your marriage and family, creating a rhythm of seeking God's presence and guidance at every turn.

Priscilla and Aquila also remind us that praying boldly for your family means interceding for your children, relatives, and future generations. It's about leaving a spiritual legacy of love, faith, and prayer. In this way, you can influence generations to come, just as the reverberations of Priscilla and Aquila's prayers are still felt today.

Let's look at the power of gratitude in bold prayer. Acknowledging and thanking God for His continued blessings and answered prayers cultivates an atmosphere of faith and hope in your home. This practice honors God and strengthens your confidence in His faithfulness in all seasons of life.

Priscilla and Aquila's journey wasn't without its challenges, but their commitment to pray boldly through every trial is an inspiring model. When faced with difficulties, they didn't retreat in fear or doubt; they drew closer together in prayer, trusting in God's sovereignty and provision. Their example teaches us that bold prayer can sustain and propel your marriage through the most difficult times.

Using Priscilla and Aquila as inspiration, consider how you can weave bold prayer into the fabric of your marriage and family life. Begin by being honest about your needs and desires, and extend that to interceding for others around you. The impact of such prayers isn't just immediate; it has eternal significance, building a legacy of faith that will stand the test of time.

Moreover, having the courage to pray fervently means acknowledging the source of your strength. It means recognizing that the victories and progress in your relationship and family are not due to your strength, but to the power of God. This humility allows God to work miracles in and through your relationship.

Finally, the example of Priscilla and Aquila compels us. In the realm of bold prayer, community has immense power. Share your prayer needs with trusted believers, join prayer groups, and actively participate in the spiritual life of your local church. When you do, you'll find encouragement, support, and a shared sense of purpose that mirrors the vibrant community life of the early church.

In conclusion, praying boldly for your marriage and family, inspired by Priscilla and Aquila, is a journey of faith, hope, and love. It invites God's power into your relationship to transform your lives and those around you. Embrace this call with an open heart and watch your marriage become a testimony to the power of prayer, impacting generations to come.

Jimmy and Rosalynn Carter Prays Boldly

In the grand narrative of bold prayers that have shaped history, the story of Jimmy and Rosalynn Carter stands as a beacon of hope and testament to the power of prayer in marriage and family life.[14] This couple, whose journey has spanned more than seven decades, offers profound insights into the importance of praying boldly for one's marriage and family.

---

[14] Rosalynn Carter: A Mental Health Advocate's Journey. https://wolrdinfotoday.com/rosalynn-carter-a-mental-health-advocates-journey/

[15] Larson, Alina. "Jimmy Carter: How Prayer Sustained Him." *Guideposts*, 5 Nov. 2010, guideposts.org/prayer/holiday-prayers/jimmy-carter-how-prayer-sustained-him/. Accessed 4 May 2024.

Bold Prayers

Their story begins in a small town where their paths crossed early in life. But it wasn't just a budding romance that grew; along with their love for one another, a shared commitment to prayer blossomed.[15] This commitment became the foundation upon which they built their lives together, navigating the complexities of marriage, family, and even the challenging terrain of political life.

Before embarking on his journey as president, Jimmy Carter, with Rosalynn by his side, understood the power of seeking divine guidance. Together, they made prayer a central part of their daily lives, embodying the principle that bold prayers can lead to bold results. Their prayers were not just petitions for personal gain, but fervent requests for strength, wisdom, and guidance to effectively serve others.

Throughout his political career, Jimmy faced numerous challenges that would have overwhelmed anyone without spiritual support. During these times, the Carters turned to prayer not as a last resort, but as a first response. They prayed boldly, with confidence and expectation, not out of naivety, but out of a deep belief in the transforming power of prayer.

Equally committed to public service, Rosalynn faced her own challenges. Together they faced the scrutiny of public life, the stress of leadership, and the strain these forces can place on marriage and family. Yet through it all, their faith and practice of boldly praying for their marriage and family remained unshaken.

They didn't just pray for the easy times, but also for the days of doubt and uncertainty. They understood that to pray boldly meant to ask for blessings, the strength to endure trials, the grace to navigate conflicts, and the wisdom to make decisions that are in line with God's will.

A remarkable aspect of the Carters' prayer life is their belief in the power of praying together. This united prayer front has been a source of strength and unity, illustrating the biblical principle that "where two or three are gathered in my name, there am I in the midst of them. Their example underscores the importance of mutual support in prayer within a marriage and how a shared spiritual practice can strengthen the bonds of love and partnership.

Their courageous prayers went beyond personal concerns to embrace a larger vision for peace, justice, and compassion in the world. This outward focus reflects a deep understanding of the role of prayer in personal transformation and social change. The Carters' prayers for their family extended to their global human family, demonstrating a comprehensive approach to prayer that seeks the good of all.

In times of crisis, such as when Jimmy faced health challenges, their family's faith was tested. But it was during these trials that the power of their courageous prayers was most evident. Their prayers for healing, comfort, and peace echoed through the corridors of hospitals, into the hearts of their family members, and to the ears of the Divine.

Their testimony is a powerful reminder that prayer is not passive, but a dynamic and courageous act of faith. It requires the courage to ask for what seems impossible, the patience to wait in expectation, and the strength to accept the outcome, understanding that sometimes the answer may be different from what was hoped for.

The legacy of Jimmy and Rosalynn Carter's prayerful life is a treasure trove of wisdom for modern marriages and families. It teaches us that bold prayer can lead to extraordinary results and reinforces the truth that at the heart of every outstanding achievement lies a foundation of faith and prayer.

Reflecting on her story, one can't help but be inspired to adopt a similar attitude of bold prayer in one's own life. Whether navigating the joys and challenges of marriage, the complexities of family life, or the demands of public service, the Carters' example is a guiding light.

So as we consider the role of courageous prayer in our lives, let the journey of Jimmy and Rosalynn Carter remind us that when we unite in prayer with faith, patience, and expectation, we open ourselves to the possibility of divine guidance, strength, and, ultimately, transformation.

Ultimately, their story is not just about the power of courageous prayer; it's a call to action. It encourages us to approach our relationships and challenges with bold faith, believing in the transformative power of prayer to renew our marriages, strengthen our families, and impact the world. So let her example encourage us to pray boldly, expecting great things from a great God.

Chapter 5 Discussion Questions

As we explore the concept of bold prayer for our marriage and family, it's important to consider how this act of faith can bring transformation to our immediate relationships and extend its impact to our family dynamics and beyond. To help you introspect and apply the principles of bold prayer to your marriage and family, we have compiled some questions that will inspire and encourage you to nurture your relationships with faith.

1. **Reflect on the example of Priscilla and Aquila.** How do their actions inspire you to approach prayer with more courage and faith in your marriage? Think about how their mutual support and shared spiritual goals can serve as a model for inviting God's presence into your relationship.

2. **Consider the heartwarming journey of Jimmy and Rosalynn Carter.** In what ways do their prayers reflect a commitment not only to their personal relationship, but also to the broader well-being of their family and community? How can their legacy motivate you to seek bold prayers that encompass personal fulfillment and social contribution?

3. **Examine your own prayer habits.** In what areas of your marriage and family life have you been reluctant to pray boldly? Is there a particular fear or limitation that is holding you back? Challenge yourself to identify one bold prayer you can commit to this week that seeks growth, healing, or blessing in your family dynamic.

Prayer is a powerful tool for building stronger bonds, nurturing love, and fostering an environment of mutual respect and understanding within the family. By deeply exploring these questions, you'll take an important step toward unlocking a more vibrant, faith-filled future for you and your loved ones. Let's embrace the power of prayer with openness, expectation, and courage.

Take Action

As we immerse ourselves in the stories of Priscilla and Aquilla and Jimmy and Rosalynn Carter, we gain a deep sense of boldness in prayer, especially when it comes to the sacred realms of marriage and family. The stories of these inspiring figures don't just serve to educate; they call us to action. It's up to us to translate that boldness into our daily lives and channel their strength in our quest for spiritual fulfillment within the family unit. Embracing bold prayer for our marriages and families means stepping into a place of vulnerability and hope, asking not only for our desires, but for the flourishing of our loved ones.

First and foremost, identify the areas in your marriage and family life that deeply need divine intervention. It may be harmony, it may be understanding, or it may be getting through a difficult time together. Just as Priscilla and Aquilla worked together in faith for the advancement of the early Christian communities, let your prayers encompass the well-being and growth of your family unit, making your requests with sincerity and an open heart to receive.

Then commit to a daily practice of boldly praying together with your spouse or family. This unity in prayer strengthens your bonds and creates a shared spiritual journey toward the blessings you seek. "The power of prayer is amplified when it is done in the presence of agreement and faith. Allow these moments to be a time of openness, where each member has the space to express his or her prayers and aspirations.

Beyond personal and collective prayers, include acts of service within your family as a physical manifestation of your prayers. As James reminds us, "Faith alone, if it is not accompanied by action, is dead. Let your actions toward one another reflect the bold prayers you've lifted up, embodying patience, kindness, and understanding. Through these actions, your family will become a living testimony of faith in action, demonstrating the transformative power of bold prayer for your marriage and family.

Finally, let this journey of bold prayer for your family and marriage be marked by ongoing gratitude. Recognize and celebrate each step forward as an answer to prayer, no matter how small. This attitude of thanksgiving will foster a positive spirit within the family and strengthen your faith in the power of prayer. As you journey along this transformative path, let your bold prayers become the cornerstone of a thriving, spiritually enriched family life that stands as a beacon of hope and love.

Chapter 6:
Praying Bold for Strong Leadership, Wisdom, and Commitment to Prayer

In the journey towards spiritual renewal, we must recognize the critical role of leadership. Praying for strong leadership isn't just wishful thinking; it's an act of faith that calls for the divine guidance and courage needed to guide communities through turbulent times. Leadership steeped in wisdom and committed to prayer can transform individuals and entire societies.

Consider for a moment the stories of those who have led with conviction, often in the midst of uncertainty and opposition. These stories aren't just historical footnotes, but testimonies to the power of courageous prayer. As we delve into the essence of praying for leadership, we come to understand the interconnectedness of leadership, wisdom, and a prayerful life.

Leadership requires more than charisma or authority; it requires wisdom, which often comes from a deep connection to the divine through prayer. When we boldly pray for wisdom, we ask for knowledge and the discernment to apply that knowledge in ways that bring about positive change. It's a prayer for the insight to navigate the complexities of human dynamics and the foresight to see the implications of our decisions.

A commitment to prayer is not a passive act, but a dynamic engagement with the divine that shapes our inner being and prepares us for the challenges of leadership. Such a commitment fosters the resilience that is essential in leadership. It equips us with the spiritual strength to face trials, make difficult decisions, and stand firm in our convictions.

As we pray boldly for steadfast leadership, let's remember the example of Daniel. Daniel remained steadfast in his commitment to prayer in the face of potential danger. Daniel's story is not just about the courage to pray in difficult times; it's a profound testament to how a prayer-filled life can encourage us to lead with integrity and wisdom.

Another example of courageous prayer, Benjamin Mays, demonstrated that leadership infused with wisdom and a commitment to prayer can inspire movements that transcend individual lifetimes. His life teaches us that our prayers for leadership should also be prayers for the courage to act on our convictions, even when doing so may not be popular or safe.

Praying for leadership is, by its very nature, an act of hope. It's a declaration of our belief in God's potential to work through human vessels to accomplish His will on earth. Let us not be afraid to pray ambitiously, asking for leaders who are not only decisive and strong, but also deeply rooted in their spiritual practice.

The wisdom we seek in these prayers is not just the ability to do things right, but to do the right things. It's a plea for moral clarity to distinguish between the urgent and the important, the temporal and the eternal.

Bold Prayers

In our commitment to prayer, we find the strength to lead and the grace to follow. Leadership, after all, isn't just about the person at the top; it's about the collective journey toward a shared vision. It's about recognizing that authentic leadership often involves serving, listening, and empowering others.

As we pray for solid leadership, let's also be willing to be the answer to our prayers. Let's embody the wisdom we seek, stand up for the values we hold dear, and cultivate a prayer life that sustains us through the ups and downs of the leadership journey.

Fostering a culture of courageous prayer in our communities can lead to transformation beyond individual leadership. It creates an environment where wisdom is valued, and a robust commitment to prayer strengthens our collective efforts.

Remember, the quality of our leadership is a direct reflection of the depth of our prayer life. When we cultivate a personal and corporate commitment to prayer, we open ourselves to divine guidance and empowerment that can elevate our leadership beyond our natural abilities.

As we move forward, let's commit to praying with conviction for our current and future leaders. Let's earnestly seek divine wisdom, believing that through our bold prayers we can help shape a future of compassionate, courageous, and wise leadership.

Finally, let this chapter be a call to prayer and an invitation to action. Let's live out the principles we pray for and demonstrate through our lives the transformative power of leadership guided by divine wisdom and an unwavering commitment to prayer. Through our bold prayers and corresponding actions, we can indeed help usher in a renewal that reflects the hope and resilience embodied in the story of Nehemiah.

In closing, let the essence of our prayers for leadership reflect the profound realization that the strength of our communities, nations, and the global village rests not only in the hands of those who lead, but in the collective will of those who boldly pray for divine guidance, wisdom, and an unwavering commitment to serve. It's a journey we are all invited to share, one prayer at a time.

Daniel Prays Boldly for Strong Leadership, Wisdom, and Commitment to Prayer

At the heart of one of the most challenging stories in the ancient texts, we discover a man named Daniel. His story is more than a testament to survival in the face of adversity; it's a master class in seeking divine wisdom and bold leadership through committed prayer. Daniel's boldness in praying for sound leadership and wisdom holds profound lessons for us today as we navigate the complexities and challenges of our own lives.

Daniel's context was far from the comfort zones we know. He lived under oppressive regimes, yet he thrived because his spirit was grounded in something deeper than the temporary power structures around him. Daniel knew the importance of seeking divine guidance, not only for personal enlightenment, but also for the good of his community and the leaders above him.

Prayer was Daniel's strategic tool for navigating complex political landscapes. His commitment to daily prayer was not a byproduct of time or a lack of urgency in his life. On the contrary, Daniel prayed boldly because he understood that wisdom and strong leadership are critical to the health and well-being of society, and these are gifts that only the divine can bestow in full measure.

When Daniel prayed for leadership, he wasn't just hoping for better rulers or more favorable conditions. He was acknowledging the sovereign power over all kings and kingdoms and inviting divine intervention and influence in human affairs. This profound truth reminds us that we, too, should look beyond the immediacy of our circumstances in our prayers, seeking the imprint of divine wisdom on the fabric of our governance structures.

Wisdom, as Daniel well knew, is essential to leadership, but it is not a common commodity. It requires a depth of insight, understanding, and foresight far beyond human capacity. Daniel's prayers for wisdom acknowledged this gap and sought divine filling. In doing so, he positioned himself and those he influenced as vessels through which divine guidance and wisdom could flow.

A commitment to prayer, as seen in Daniel's life, is one of the most overlooked aspects of the quest for sound leadership and wisdom. Daniel's consistent devotion to prayer was not just a routine, it was a lifeline. It was his connection to an unchanging source of strength and guidance in a turbulent world. For Daniel, a commitment to prayer was not optional; it was essential.

This unwavering commitment to prayer exemplifies a boldness that transcends human courage, especially in times of need. It demonstrates a trust in the divine that can seem counterintuitive, especially when immediate results are not visible. Daniel's story encourages us to persevere in prayer, knowing that our bold requests for sound guidance and wisdom are not in vain.

Daniel shows us that prayer is also an act of resistance. It resists the narratives of despair and powerlessness and affirms the role of a higher power in human affairs. This act of faith does not deny reality, but confronts it with a greater truth: divine wisdom and guidance can have a significant impact on our world, shaping leadership that is consistent with justice and righteousness.

Daniel's prayers were not self-centered. He prayed for the welfare of his captors and for the prosperity of the kingdom that held him captive, demonstrating an extraordinary level of insight. His requests for effective leadership and wisdom went beyond personal or short-term gain to include the welfare of all people, including those who did not share his beliefs or values.

The impact of Daniel's recorded prayers was profound. They catalyzed change, brought insight to kings, and influenced the course of nations. This historical account underscores the potential of prayer to produce significant results, not only in spiritual realms, but also in tangible, earthly realities.

As we reflect on Daniel's life, we find an application-rich model for our prayer lives. First, like Daniel, we must recognize our dependence on divine wisdom and guidance in every area of our lives, including our desire for strong and wise leadership. This recognition is the first step in cultivating a courageous prayer life that dares to ask for what seems impossible.

Second, Daniel teaches us that our commitment to prayer should be unwavering, rooted not in our circumstances but in our relationship with the divine. Such a commitment will carry us through seasons of abundance and need, influencing not only our personal growth but also the well-being of our communities.

Finally, the story of Daniel challenges us to see our prayers as instruments of transformation in the world. By boldly praying for wisdom and strong leadership, we align ourselves with divine purposes and become conduits through which God's will can be manifested in our societies.

As we draw inspiration from Daniel's example, let us approach our prayer lives with renewed vigor and expectation. Let's be bold in our petitions for sound leadership and divine wisdom, knowing that such prayers are hopeful aspirations and powerful tools for shaping the world around us.

Like Daniel, may we dare to pray boldly, trust deeply, and live wisely, recognizing that our most powerful actions are our prayers. In this way, we can hope to see the transformation of our leadership, our communities, and ultimately our world, based on the unwavering wisdom and guidance that comes from above.

Dr. Benjamin Mays Prays for Strong Leadership, Wisdom, and Commitment to Prayer

Few figures in American history have embodied the principles of strong leadership, wisdom, and a deep commitment to prayer like Benjamin Mays. His life and work offer profound lessons for anyone seeking guidance in navigating the complexities of leadership in any arena - spiritual, political, or social. As we delve into the story of Benjamin Mays' journey, we find invaluable insights for our spiritual growth and leadership paths.

Mays' philosophy of leadership was deeply intertwined with his faith. He believed that the essence of sound leadership was not simply to command respect or wield power, but to serve others with humility and integrity. This perspective is especially relevant today, when leadership is more about personal gain than serving the common good. Benjamin Mays' life teaches us that prayer is not a passive act, but a powerful tool for nurturing leadership qualities within ourselves.

One of the most compelling aspects of Benjamin Mays' approach to leadership was his wisdom. He understood that true wisdom comes not from accumulated knowledge alone, but from a deep connection with the Divine. Mays' commitment to prayer was a testament to his belief in seeking divine guidance for every decision. His example encourages us to turn to worship not only in times of crisis, but as a constant source of strength and wisdom.

Benjamin Mays' influence on civil rights leaders, especially Martin Luther King Jr., underscores the transformative power of a prayerful life. King often spoke of Mays' influence on his approach to leadership, emphasizing the importance of prayer in the struggle for justice and equality. This mentoring relationship exemplifies Benjamin Mays' legacy, inspiring a new generation of leaders with his wisdom and spiritual commitment.

Benjamin Mays' life is a beacon for those who seek to cultivate strong leadership. He reminds us that leadership is not about the position we hold, but about the disposition we embody. True leaders are those who demonstrate resilience, wisdom, and a servant's heart through their commitment to prayer and spiritual growth.

Benjamin Mays' unwavering commitment to prayer underscores the importance of a solid spiritual foundation. In his view, prayer is the bedrock upon which character and leadership are built. This principle is especially relevant in times of uncertainty and change. When the ground seems to be shifting beneath us, our prayer life can provide the stability and guidance we desperately need.

Another lesson from the life of Benjamin Mayes is the power of visionary leadership. He dared to imagine a world beyond the immediate reality of segregation and inequality. Through prayer, he sought divine insight to guide his actions to bring about this new vision. His example teaches us that as emerging leaders, our vision should not be limited by our current circumstances, but expanded through our communion with God.

Mays also demonstrated the importance of consistency in practicing a commitment to prayer. Prayer was not a sporadic endeavor for him, but a daily discipline. This habitual return to prayer equipped him with the strength and wisdom necessary to face the challenges of his time. Through Mays's example, we learn that our spiritual practices, including prayer, must be woven into our daily lives.

In addition, Benjamin Mays' life exemplifies the virtue of courage in leadership. His reliance on prayer strengthened his resolve to stand firm in his convictions even in the face of opposition. For those of us who seek to make bold changes in our lives or communities, Mays's courage, rooted in his faith, offers encouragement to move forward despite the obstacles.

Another key takeaway is the humility that Mays demonstrated in his leadership. Despite his significant accomplishments and influence, he remained grounded in his faith and identity as a servant of God and humanity. This humility, cultivated through his commitment to prayer, kept him from succumbing to arrogance or pride. It's an important reminder that authentic leadership is not defined by how high one rises, but by how low one is willing to stoop to lift others.

Mays also understood the importance of mentorship and community in cultivating strong leaders. His relationship with King exemplified how wisdom and values can be passed on through personal connection and shared prayer. This aspect of Benjamin Mays's life encourages us to seek out mentors who embody the principles of strong leadership and spiritual depth to which we aspire.

Finally, Mays' legacy calls us to action. It's not enough to admire his life and teachings from afar; we are challenged to embody these principles in our own lives. Whether leading a family, a community, or an organization, we can apply Mays's wisdom, commitment to prayer, and servant leadership to make a tangible difference.

In conclusion, Benjamin Mays' life offers a blueprint for those who seek to combine strong leadership with deep spirituality. Through his unwavering commitment to prayer, deep wisdom, and dedication to serving others, Mays has left a legacy that transcends time. His story encourages us to pursue our leadership journey with humility, courage, and an ever-deepening relationship with the Divine. Let us take these lessons to heart and strive to embody them in our daily lives, knowing that all things are possible through prayer.

As we reflect on Benjamin May's rich life and its implications for our journey, we are reminded of the transformative power of prayer in cultivating leadership. May we approach our leadership roles with the same spirit of service, commitment to prayer, and dedication to cultivating wisdom that Mays exemplified throughout his remarkable life.

Chapter Six Discussions

As we dig into the heart of our journey to pray with authority, seek divine wisdom, and cultivate a committed prayer life, we need to reflect on the powerful examples in this chapter. Daniel and Dr. Benjamin Mays, pillars of solid leadership and commitment to prayer, have set patterns that we can confidently emulate. As we discuss these aspects, several critical points emerge:

1. **Understanding the Foundation of Strong Leadership:** Strong leadership isn't just about making tough decisions; it's about making those decisions rooted in prayer and wisdom. Think about how both Daniel and Dr. Benjamin Mays approached leadership. Consider what it means to lead not from a place of power, but from a place of prayer and submission to divine guidance. How can we apply these principles to our contexts in our families, workplaces, or communities?

2. **The Role of Wisdom in Our Daily Walk:** Wisdom isn't just knowledge or intelligence. A discerning heart knows the right course of action, guided by God's hand. Think about how the characters discussed have exemplified seeking wisdom through prayer. How can we actively seek divine wisdom in our daily decisions and challenges?

3. **Committing to a Vibrant Prayer Life:** Both Daniel and Dr. Benjamin Mays demonstrated an unwavering commitment to prayer, understanding its power and necessity. This commitment often requires discipline and a conscious decision to prioritize prayer in the midst of the busyness of life. How can we foster this commitment in our own lives and make prayer a non-negotiable part of our daily routine?

Incorporating these elements into our journey can transform how we pray and how we live, lead, and navigate the complexities of life. Let's accept the call to pray boldly for solid leadership, to seek divine wisdom earnestly, and to commit wholeheartedly to a vibrant prayer life. As we do so, we become conduits for the change we seek, empowered by the One who hears our prayers.

Building effective leadership and wisdom requires a committed prayer life. Let's pray for change and be the change through our actions, decisions and leadership.

Take Action

Action is essential in the journey of prayerfully seeking strong leadership, wisdom, and an unwavering commitment to prayer. It's not just about wishing for change or longing for deeper spiritual depths from the sidelines. It's about embodying change, becoming a vessel through which divine wisdom and leadership can manifest. As Daniel and Dr. Benjamin Mays demonstrated through their lives, our actions can deeply echo our prayers and weave them into the fabric of reality.

First, identify the leadership qualities you want to develop or support in others. Is it courage in the face of adversity, the wisdom to make tough decisions, or the humility to serve others unselfishly? Once you have a clear vision, pray for it. But don't stop there. Seek out resources, mentors, and communities that align with these qualities. Remember, prayer is dynamic; it moves us to act, to seek, and to knock on the door of opportunity with faith and determination.

Next, cultivate wisdom daily. This isn't just an accumulation of knowledge, but a discerning understanding and application of that knowledge in a way that aligns with the divine will. Make it a habit to reflect on the scriptures, seeking the wisdom that has guided countless generations. Couple this with a commitment to lifelong learning - formal education, personal reading, or engaging in meaningful conversation. Wisdom grows in the soil of an open, curious mind.

A commitment to prayer should be the thread that runs through every aspect of your life. It's not reserved for moments of crisis or the quiet of a morning routine. Integrate prayer into your daily activities, transforming mundane tasks into moments of mindfulness and connection with the divine. This can be as simple as saying a prayer of gratitude with each meal, offering prayers for guidance during meetings, or dedicating a particular activity as a prayer practice. The key is to be consistent and intentional.

Finally, let your life itself be a bold prayer. A prayer for solid leadership, wisdom, and commitment to prayer isn't just something we say; it's something we live. Let the principles you've prayed for guide you in every decision, interaction, and moment of reflection. The boldness of your prayers will only be matched by the boldness of your actions. Remember, every step you take in faith, empowered by prayer, is a step toward the renewal and rejuvenation of your life and those around you.

Chapter 7: Adapting to New Challenges

Life, as we know, isn't static. Just when we think we've got it all figured out, a new challenge emerges, beckoning us to adapt, grow, and transcend our previous limitations. These unexpected twists and turns are not obstacles, but opportunities-divinely placed chances to strengthen our prayer life and deepen our faith. The story of Nehemiah shows how he stood firm and adapted with wisdom and courage in the face of unprecedented challenges. This chapter explores how we can adapt to new challenges through prayer.

Each challenge we face is unique and requires a nuanced approach to overcome. However, the need for prayer remains constant. Whether we are dealing with personal turmoil, financial hardship, or a crisis of faith, reaching out in prayer becomes our most powerful tool. It connects us to divine guidance and provides clarity and strength in turbulent times.

Facing new challenges can leave us feeling vulnerable and exposed, testing our faith. Yet it is in these moments of vulnerability that our prayer life can truly flourish. By acknowledging our weaknesses and uncertainties in prayer, we open ourselves to God's infinite strength and wisdom-a transformative process that builds our resilience.

Adapting to new challenges requires humility. It requires acknowledging that we don't have all the answers and that our current methods are not sufficient. This humble acknowledgment isn't a sign of defeat, but an essential step toward spiritual growth. It leads us to pray for solutions and for the wisdom and insight to understand the changes that are needed.

In addition, prayer encourages us to move beyond our comfort zones by accepting new challenges. Nehemiah didn't rebuild the walls of Jerusalem by sticking to the status quo. He prayed, planned and acted decisively, stepping into uncharted territory with faith as his guide. We must trust that divine guidance will hear us and show us the way, even when we are uncertain about the path ahead.

Cooperation in prayer is another key aspect of adapting to new challenges. Nehemiah didn't take on the task of rebuilding the walls alone; he rallied the community and encouraged collective prayer and action. There's immense power in communal prayer-a shared faith that builds hope and resilience. As we face new challenges, we must seek support by sharing our burdens and victories with others in prayer.

Persistence in prayer is essential. To overcome challenges, we must pray persistently with faith and perseverance. Nehemiah's success was not instantaneous; it was the result of consistent prayer, effort, and unwavering faith over time. Similarly, we must remain committed to our prayer life, trusting that each prayer will plant a seed of change.

Adapting to new challenges also means being open to unexpected answers to our prayers. Sometimes the solution to our problem is different from what we expected or hoped for. It may require a change in direction or the letting go of something we hold dear. In these cases, our faith, nurtured through prayer, helps us accept and embrace God's plan for us.

As we face new challenges, we should pray earnestly while working hard toward our goals. This combination of divine trust and proactive effort is at the heart of every challenge we overcome. Our prayers reflect our desires and our commitment to act in faith.

It's also worth noting that adapting to new challenges often involves waiting-a time that can test our patience and resolve. However, it is in these times of waiting that our prayer life can deepen, giving us a profound sense of peace and purpose. Before rebuilding the walls of Jerusalem, Nehemiah waited, prayed fervently, and prepared diligently. Similarly, our periods of waiting are not idle time, but preparation for what's to come.

Throughout history, the most outstanding spiritual leaders have faced significant challenges with prayerful resilience. They didn't see challenges as obstacles, but as pathways to a closer relationship with God. Their lives are powerful examples that teach us that the most profound personal and community growth often comes from the most formidable challenges.

Moreover, responding to new challenges through prayer transforms us and can have a ripple effect that inspires those around us. As we face our trials with faith and grace, we become beacons of hope and resilience, encouraging others to pray in their time of need.

In the journey of faith, we must continually learn and grow. We're never alone in our struggles. With prayer as our compass, we can navigate through any storm and emerge stronger, wiser, and more connected to our divine purpose.

Likewise, as we move forward, let's take with us the lessons from the story of Nehemiah and the countless others who have demonstrated that with faith, prayer and action, no challenge is insurmountable. Through our prayerful adaptability, we can truly embody the spirit of resilience and renewal to which God calls us.

As we face new challenges, let us pray not for an easier life, but for the strength, wisdom, and courage to overcome the obstacles that come our way. For in every challenge lies an opportunity for growth, a chance to deepen our faith, and a journey toward a life of meaning, peace, and deep joy.

Chapter 8:
Being Open to Change and Growth

When we embrace change and growth, we open the windows of a stale room to let in fresh air that revitalizes and energizes us for the new possibilities ahead. We dedicate this chapter to encouraging you to embrace change, drawing inspiration from the biblical story of Nehemiah. He understood that rebuilding the walls of Jerusalem involved not only physical labor, but also spiritual renewal and community transformation.[16]

Growth often comes in the form of challenges that push us out of our comfort zones. To be open to change, we must be willing to face these challenges head-on, with faith as our foundation. Nehemiah faced opposition and ridicule; resources were scarce and the task seemed impossible. Yet his unwavering faith and openness to divine guidance catalyzed the miraculous rebuilding of the walls in just 52 days.

---

[16] Stowers, Clarence. *From Rubble to Renewal: The Nehemiah Strategy for Modern Times. Amazon*, Staten House, 22 Jan. 2024, a.co/d/bAKsDA3. Accessed 4 May 2024.

Similarly, our desire for spiritual growth and transformation requires a heart that is open to change. It means seeing each prayer as a seed of change that, when planted in the fertile ground of faith, can lead to breakthrough changes in our lives. Praying for bold breakthroughs in finances, relationships, or personal development essentially serves as a prayer for change.

Change can be scary. Human nature often leads us to seek the comfort of the familiar, even if it hinders our growth. Yet history and scripture repeatedly show us that the most profound periods of growth come from our willingness to embrace the unknown. The story of Nehemiah testifies to the power of facing the unknown with courage and conviction.

Embracing change means letting go of old habits and perspectives that no longer serve us. It means being open to new ways of thinking, praying, and living. This openness transforms our prayers from wishful thinking into dynamic conversations with the Divine, guiding us toward our purpose and potential.

Growth is an ongoing process, not a goal. It requires patience, perseverance, and above all, prayer. When we pray boldly, we open ourselves to the possibility of change, recognizing that we can shape our destiny through faith, action, and an open heart as co-creators with the Divine.

Think about the courageous prayers you've made in the past. Think about how they have led you down new paths, opened doors you never knew existed, and brought growth into your life. Your openness to change and willingness to step into the unknown, guided by faith, fueled these moments of transformation.

To cultivate openness to change, you must remain rooted in faith and connected to a community that supports and lifts you up. Nehemiah didn't rebuild the walls of Jerusalem alone; others who shared his vision helped him. Similarly, the encouragement, insights, and prayers of those around us enrich our journey of growth.

We must also remain flexible and adaptable. Just as a tree bends with the wind to avoid breaking, we must adjust our strategies and plans in response to unpredictable changes. This flexibility is a critical component of growth and a hallmark of resilient faith.

In addition, we must recognize the power of gratitude in our journey toward change and growth. Recognizing and giving thanks for each step forward, no matter how small, fuels our momentum and keeps us aligned with our higher purpose. Nehemiah consistently expressed gratitude to God, which strengthened his resolve and lifted his spirit.

In your prayers, ask not only for the strength to face change, but also for the wisdom to recognize its opportunities for growth. Trust that the lessons embedded in each challenge are stepping stones to a fuller, richer life.

Finally, remember that when you are open to change and growth, you are making a courageous act of faith. It's a statement that you trust the divine plan for your life, even when the path is unclear. Nehemiah's story didn't end with the completion of the walls; it began a new chapter for Jerusalem and its people. Likewise, each change we embrace, each step we take in faith, begins a new chapter in our lives, filled with endless possibilities for growth and transformation.

As you continue your journey, carry with you the lessons of Nehemiah- the power of prayer, the strength found in community, and the transformative potential of an open heart. Let these guide you as you navigate the complexities of life, always moving forward, always growing, and always open to the wonders that change can bring.

In conclusion, being open to change and growth isn't just an aspect of our spiritual journey; it embodies its essence. It's about constantly evolving, learning, and striving to become the best versions of ourselves in alignment with our divine purpose. So, let's embark on this journey with open hearts, ready to receive, adapt and grow. In change lies the potential for remarkable renewal, just as Nehemiah showed us, from ruin to renewal.

Chapter 9: Building on Ancient Wisdom for Modern Day Success

Every chapter of this journey has unlocked the power of drawing from the past to redefine our present and future. The stories of ancient figures and modern leaders alike have illustrated a timeless truth: combining ancient wisdom with the audacity to pray boldly creates a formula for unparalleled success in our lives.

Let's recap what this blending of the ages means for us today. At its core, this fusion isn't about mirroring rituals or echoing ancient prayers. It's about understanding that the principles underlying those prayers-faith, resilience, and the audacity to seek divine intervention in our boldest dreams-are as relevant today as they were centuries ago. We have seen how figures like Abraham and Hannah, and leaders like Martin Luther King and Rosa Parks, have used these principles to bring about transformative change.

The question is whether these ancient strategies can work in our modern age. The evidence is clear: they can, and they do. The real question is how to effectively integrate this wisdom into our daily lives so that our prayers aren't just words, but catalysts for action and change.

One practical step we have explored is the practice of courageous prayer. It's not about the volume of our voice, but the magnitude of our faith. Praying boldly means stepping out of our comfort zones and asking for big things-breakthroughs in our finances, miracles in our marriages, unprecedented success in our endeavors-with an unwavering belief that they are attainable.

Another critical lesson is overcoming the fear that often accompanies asking for more. Hannah's story illustrates this poignantly. Despite her despair, she prayed for a child, a request that seemed impossible but was granted. Like Hannah, when we face our fears and present our deepest desires to the Divine, we align ourselves with the possibility of achieving what seems unattainable.

Trust and expectation should be the twin pillars of our prayer life. Elijah's story reminds us to anticipate outcomes not as feasible, but as divinely possible. This mindset shift isn't trivial. It requires a deep, often challenging reevaluation of our faith and our understanding of what prayer can accomplish.

Importantly, these ancient principles call us to action, not passivity. Nehemiah didn't just pray; he planned, petitioned the king, and actively participated in rebuilding the walls of Jerusalem. His story underscores the importance of combining prayer with effort to bring about desired change.

As we navigate the uncertainties of our times, Esther's wisdom teaches us the importance of timing, courage and advocacy, not just for our personal gain, but for the greater good. Like Esther, we're called to be bold and stand up for what's right, even at great personal risk.

Adapting to new challenges and being open to change and growth are also critical components of this process. These aren't just strategies for success; they are prerequisites. The world is constantly evolving, and our ability to respond with agility and an open heart to God's direction will determine our ability to thrive.

So as we conclude this narrative, let's consider how we can embody these teachings. It's about more than individual success; it's about fostering a community that believes in the power of prayer, supports one another on their spiritual journeys, and works together toward a brighter future.

The steps for those who wish to deepen their prayer life are clear. It begins with a commitment to pray boldly, to educate ourselves in the wisdom of the ancients, and to apply these principles with a heart ready for transformation.

Let us then walk this path not as passive observers, but as active participants in a story much larger than ourselves. Let's weave ancient wisdom into our daily lives, allowing it to shape our decisions, guide our steps, and lead us into a future filled with promise and success.

In conclusion, the journey from ruin to renewal requires faith, action, and a willingness to learn from the past. By building on ancient wisdom, we honor those who have gone before us and pave the way for a future where bold prayer and unwavering faith unlock new dimensions of success in our personal lives and in our communities.

As we close this chapter, let's look forward to the next steps in our journey. May we be inspired by the stories we've shared, motivated by the successes we've seen, and encouraged by the knowledge that with faith and action, nothing is beyond our reach.

Appendix A: Resources for Further Study

The journey to spiritually rebuild one's life, much like the experience of Nehemiah, is both challenging and enriching. As we close this chapter of our exploration, it is crucial to understand that the journey doesn't end here. The transformation witnessed in these pages is only the beginning. We've curated a selection of resources to further guide and support you on this pilgrimage. These resources are stepping stones to deepen your understanding, refine your prayer strategies, and continue your growth in faith and spiritual maturity.

Books

Immerse yourself in a collection of works that reflect the themes and lessons presented in our discussions. Each book has been carefully selected to expand your knowledge and inspire you to live a life of bold prayer and unwavering faith.

- Prayer: Experiencing Awe and Intimacy with God by Timothy Keller[17] - A profound exploration of the

---

[17] (Keller, Prayer: Experiencing Awe and Intimacy with God 2016)

power of prayer, with practical guidance for making prayer a reality in your daily life.

- The Circle Maker: Praying Circles Around Your Biggest Dreams and Greatest Fears by Mark Batterson[18] - Learn about the legacy of Honi the Circle Maker and how courageous prayers can lead to extraordinary results.

- Fervent: A Woman's Battle Plan to Serious, Specific and Strategic Prayer by Priscilla Shirer[19] - A compelling call to arms for women to embrace prayer as a battlefield strategy.

---

[18] The Circle Maker: Praying Circles Around Your Biggest Dreams and Greatest Fears | World's Biggest Leveled Book Database | Readu. https://readu.io/book/6zjkd66Mmx/the-circle-maker-praying-circles-around-your-biggest-dreams-and-greatest-fears/

[19] Fervent: A Woman's Battle Plan to Serious, Specific, and Strategic Prayer by Priscilla Shirer · OverDrive: ebooks, audiobooks, and more for libraries and schools. https://search.overdrive.com/media/2288024/fervent

[20] "The Prayer Warrior on Apple Podcasts." *Apple Podcasts*, 7 Aug. 2023, podcasts.apple.com/us/podcast/the-prayer-warrior/id1681961863. Accessed 4 May 2024.

[21] "Think Biblically: Conversations on Faith & Culture on Apple Podcasts." *Apple Podcasts*, 3 May 2024, podcasts.apple.com/us/podcast/think-biblically-conversations-on-faith-culture/id1300837524. Accessed 4 May 2024.

Podcasts

In today's fast-paced world, podcasts serve as an accessible medium for cultivating knowledge and inspiration on the go. Here are a few recommendations that combine instruction and encouragement, tailored for anyone looking to strengthen their prayer life.

- The Prayer Warrior Podcast[20] - Weekly episodes focused on motivating and training believers to pray with courage and effectiveness.

- Think Biblically: Conversations on Faith & Culture [21] - A weekly podcast that offers Christian perspectives on some of the most important issues facing the church and culture today. In each episode, hosts Scott Rae and Sean McDowell - professors at Biola University's Talbot School of Theology - draw on biblical wisdom and insights from guest experts as they explore how Christians can engage thoughtfully and faithfully with cultural trends and current events. Engage with stories of faith and prayer from around the world, highlighting the diversity and unity of prayer across cultures and contexts.

Communities

Remember that the journey of spiritual renewal and growth is not meant to be traveled alone. Connecting with a community can provide support, insight, and encouragement. Look for local prayer groups or online forums dedicated to the practice of courageous prayer. Platforms such as the Mars Hill Baptist Church Facebook group can be excellent places to connect with like-minded people.

Finally, let this book not be an endpoint, but a gateway. Let the lessons, stories, and strategies discussed be the foundation upon which you build a towering edifice of faith, action, and transformation. With these resources and the unwavering spirit of bold prayer, step forward into a future ripe with potential and promise. The path ahead is illuminated by the lessons of the past and the bright hope of tomorrow. Go forward with confidence, and let your prayers be as bold as your faith.

Appendix B: Reflection Questions for Personal or Group Study

Embarking on a journey through "Bold Prayers" not only invites us to explore the transformative power of bold prayers but also challenges us to reflect deeply on our own spiritual paths. This appendix serves as a guide for reflecting on your personal growth and the collective journey of your study group. As you sincerely engage with these questions, you may discover facets of your faith and prayer life that are waiting to be awakened or nurtured.

Individual Reflection

1. Consider the story of Nehemiah and the immense challenges he faced. What personal "rubble" in your life seems insurmountable, and how can Nehemiah's example inspire you to approach it with faith and determination?

2. In your prayer life, identify a time when you prayed for something with boldness. What was the result, and how did it affect your relationship with God?

3. Think about a time when fear kept you from asking for something important in prayer. What steps can you take to overcome such fears and move forward?

4. Prayer is often a private endeavor, but corporate prayer can also be powerful. How can you incorporate more corporate prayer into your life, and what benefits do you see it bringing to your spiritual community?

5. Consider the idea of praying for bold breakthroughs in areas such as finances, relationships, or personal development. What area of your life needs the most breakthrough, and how can you begin to pray boldly for it?

Group Study Discussion

1. Share personal experiences of bold prayer with the group. Have any prayers been answered in unexpected ways? Discuss the impact of these experiences on the faith of each group member.

2. Share thoughts about the challenges of maintaining a consistent and deep prayer life in the face of modern distractions. How can group members help each other prioritize prayer?

3. Discuss the balance between accepting God's will in prayer results and persisting in prayer for something deeply desired. How can one find peace in unanswered prayer?

4. Consider the role of humility and surrender in prayer. Share examples of how surrendering to God's plan revealed results far beyond personal expectations.

5. As a group, identify a common goal or challenge for which you can commit to pray boldly together. Plan how you will support this

corporate prayer effort and track its progress and impact on the group.

As you work through these reflection questions, either alone or with your group, let them lead you to deeper insights into your spiritual journey. Whether you're seeking to rebuild your life, longing for profound change, or wanting to strengthen your relationship with God, let the act of courageous prayer open new avenues for growth and transformation. May your reflections lead you to a place of renewed faith and strengthened commitment to walk in close communion with God.

Appendix C:
Templates for Personal Prayer

Embarking on a journey of personal growth and spiritual rebuilding, much like Nehemiah, requires sincere prayer and introspection. It's through sincere conversation with God that we invite miraculous transformation into our lives.[22] The templates provided here aim to catalyze a deeper, more profound connection through prayer. Whether you're a seasoned believer or someone just beginning to explore the realms of prayerful communication, these templates serve as stepping stones to a more engaged and fulfilling prayer life.

Template 1: Prayer for Personal Growth

Heavenly Father, I stand before you today acknowledging my need for growth and development in areas both seen and unseen. This prayer is a powerful tool that can guide me on my journey and help me unfold into the fullest expression of who I'm meant to be. It illuminates the pathways of wisdom and understanding and gives me the

---

[22] Prayer is not just a conversation with the divine | Prayers Online. https://www.prayersonline.in/blog/tags/prayer-is-not-just-a-conversation-with-the-divine

courage to accept the challenges that facilitate my growth. Amen.

Template 2: Prayer for Overcoming Challenges

Dear Lord, I bring you the challenges that weigh heavily on my heart. I trust in your boundless strength and wisdom to guide me through these trials. Please grant me the resilience of Nehemiah, so that I may not falter, but instead rise stronger in faith and action. In your loving embrace I seek refuge and strength to overcome. Amen.

Template 3: Prayer for Wisdom and Guidance

Heavenly Father, source of all wisdom, I seek your guidance as I navigate the complexities of life. Grant me the clarity and discernment to make decisions that are consistent with your divine will. Teach me, O Lord, to listen intently for your voice amidst the clamor of the world, so that I may walk steadfastly in the path you have laid out for me. Amen.

Template 4: Prayer for Family and Loved Ones

Gracious God, I lift up my family and loved ones to your tender care. Bless them with your protecting grace and fill their lives with peace, love, and joy. May our bonds strengthen and support one another as we continue our collective and individual spiritual journeys. May our home be a haven of faith, understanding, and mutual respect. Amen.

Template 5: Prayer for Leadership and Influence

Mighty Counselor, I seek your guidance as a leader and influencer in my community. Instill in me the virtues of humility, wisdom, and compassion so that I may lead with integrity and inspire those around me to synergize their efforts to build a better future. May my actions reflect Your divine love and serve as a beacon of hope. Amen.

As you embark on this journey of prayer, remember that these templates are not rigid formulas, but rather starting points for your personal dialogue with the Divine. They are designed to be flexible, allowing you to adapt and modify them as inspired by your own experiences, needs, and revelations. This flexibility encourages personalization, making the process more relatable and meaningful. Embrace this opportunity to enrich your prayer life, knowing that each word you whisper in faith is a step toward spiritual renewal and transformation.

Made in the USA
Columbia, SC
26 September 2024